unwritten:

"I'm so glad that Unwritten *has been written. This book, full of small tips and major insights, can change the way you think about everyday choices as well as about significant life decisions. Jofi's candid voice and personal stories will help you find your authentic voice and chart your life story."*

—Dr. Tal Ben-Shahar
Author of *Happier*

"Jofi's introspection into what makes a happy and fulfilling life will give you the keys to find your own path. This light, profound, fun book will warm your heart and provide a new perspective on what you truly want in life."

—Christine Comaford
Leadership and Culture Coach
New York Times bestselling author of
Rules for Renegades and *Smart Tribes*

"Jofi is authentic and honest, with a strong drive to be a positive force in the world. This book is Jofi in pure form. If the sign of a good leader is to preach by example, this book is a great example that certainly opens the door to Jofi's soul. He asks a fundamental question to all of us: What would you do if you had all the money and time in the world? We can learn from Jofi's path to happiness and service. As he proves, both go together. Highly recommended."

—Juan Antonio Fernandez
Professor of Management at China Europe Business School,
Shanghai, China; author of *China CEO* and *China Entrepreneur*

"*This book is a provocative examination of the challenges we all face in this changing and competitive world. Jofi tells it as it is and by doing so, drives the reader to examine his or her purpose in life and whether there is meaning in it. He is totally convinced that if you follow your passion, everything else will fall into place. He has taken that risk, and it placed him in a sea of uncertainty. It's a gamble he describes for the reader in a straightforward and honest way.*"

—DR. JOACHIM DE POSADA
International speaker and author of
Don't Eat the Marshmallow...Yet

JOFI BALDRICH

unwritten:

A Story of
Discovering How to
Live a Happier,
More Meaningful Life

Published by Advantage, Charleston, South Carolina.
Member of Advantage Media Group.

ADVANTAGE is a registered trademark and the Advantage colophon is a trademark of Advantage Media Group, Inc.

Printed in the United States of America.

ISBN: 978-159932-371-8
LCCN: 2013939205

This publication is designed to provide accurate and authoritative information in regard to the subject matter covered. It is sold with the understanding that the publisher is not engaged in rendering legal, accounting, or other professional services. If legal advice or other expert assistance is required, the services of a competent professional person should be sought.

Advantage Media Group is proud to be a part of the Tree Neutral® program. Tree Neutral offsets the number of trees consumed in the production and printing of this book by taking proactive steps such as planting trees in direct proportion to the number of trees used to print books. To learn more about Tree Neutral, please visit www.treeneutral.com. To learn more about Advantage's commitment to being a responsible steward of the environment, please visit www.advantagefamily.com/green

Advantage Media Group is a publisher of business, self-improvement, and professional development books and online learning. We help entrepreneurs, business leaders, and professionals share their Stories, Passion, and Knowledge to help others Learn & Grow™. Do you have a manuscript or book idea that you would like us to consider for publishing? Please visit advantagefamily.com or call 1.866.775.1696.

To mami y papi
Thank you...for everything.

To my amazing, beautiful wife, Greta.
Thank you for believing in me, even when I didn't.

Who Is Jofi?

When most people first hear my name, Jofi, they wonder if they heard it right. Some ask me where it comes from. Others ask whether it's a Spanish name they might never have heard of before.

It's always a conversation starter.

Like everything in life, there's a story behind it. And it's part of the longer story I will tell you, the one about how I came to write this book.

My real name is José Fernando. My mom made up my nickname, Jofi, shortening both of my names and blending them together.

There's a little lesson in my unusual name. All my life I've simply been called "Jofi." Nobody calls me José or José Fernando. Even my business card reads "Jofi Baldrich." The informal has become the formal for me. I go by Jofi for everything. Unless it's a legal document that I have to sign with a lawyer or something like that, it's always Jofi. I remember that I wanted the name on my diploma from my high school, Colegio San Ignacio de Loyola in San Juan, Puerto Rico, to read Jofi Baldrich. Somebody in the school said no, it would have to be my real, full name, so I had no choice but to give in—at least back then. But no more. Ever since I've had a say in how things would be for me on my own terms as an adult, it's always been Jofi for everything I do. Best of all, and what I have always thought was especially cool about this name is that it's all mine. I am the only Jofi. At least, I haven't heard of anybody else named Jofi. It's pretty unique and it's spelled simply—J-O-F-I—so I like it.

On a deeper level, I think my name reflects how comfortable and confident I am in my own skin, something I've just started learning. And that is a small story that is part of the larger story about how I grew to be more comfortable with everything I wanted to do, and the paths and choices I have taken in life from childhood to adulthood.

All of that is the story told in this book, the one you now have in your hands.

An Athletic Influence

A few years ago, we sold the family insurance business. That change in circumstances made me realize many new things. I have reflected on my whole life and the way I've been living. This has included looking at who I really was and being more like my true self, the true me, the more authentic me. All of this has come about since we sold the business in 2006. It has given me time to reflect on things, along with a new freedom I have never felt before. It has taken me on a new path of self-discovery.

I've always been very athletic. In fact, I come from a family of athletes. My dad was an excellent athlete and a very good basketball referee. At one time in his life he was probably considered one of the best basketball referees in the world. He's been to the Olympics, to Mundobasket, the Pan American Games, the Central American Games, and many other major athletic events the world over. He became well known and recognized because of it. In my own son's basketball game, just the other day, somebody came up to me and asked if I were my dad's son. This man used to ref with my dad more than thirty years ago. He told me, "Well, send my best to your dad and tell him he's the best ref in the world." My father has always been well respected. He's someone people remember long after meeting him. I look a lot like him, but being like him is even more important to me.

My father tried out as a basketball referee for the National Basketball Association (NBA). There is a great story behind that, but that is for another book. The main thing is that I'm very proud of him; he's a very good athlete. A major part of his success is that he has always liked to win. I was raised in a family in which everybody played sports and was always very competitive. Our competitiveness and desire to always be at our personal best—and at our best as a family—flowed into the business world, when I worked with my dad in our family's insurance company.

That way of life impacted me deeply and in a positive way and has made me who I am. Yet, as with everything regarding families, there are many sides to this sense of intense competition. Looking back at all of it, I feel that I have settled my emotional debt in the family business. There are times when working in the family business is the logical thing to do, the "why not?"

FOLLOWING THE FAMILY BUSINESS

It's not that I regret the work we did together, but my experience makes me wonder if being a part of the family business was the path I really wanted to take. Was going into the family business a decision I had really thought about carefully and decided, "Yes, this is what I want to do"? My take on this now is that I had the time to reflect on my decision only after we'd sold the business.

That was when I realized I could do anything I wanted to do. The things I had put off doing because of family responsibility, because of being the good son, I can do now. I felt for the first time that I could make decisions on my own, without worrying about what others were thinking or worrying about disappointing anyone. It was a difficult decision for me and at times it felt lonely and scary. I had not faced a situation like that before, but with the support of my family and friends, I was able to make the right decision for me. The choice I made is the main reason for writing the book you now have in your hands. I want to share my journey with others so they can learn from what I went through. Hopefully, this will make it a little easier for others if they find themselves on the same journey.

I want to share my journey with others
so they can learn from what I went through.

I think a lot of people have gone or are going through what I'm going through, especially with their family businesses. It's great if your grandfather started a business and your dad followed the business, and you and your son did too. That's a nice story to hear, the kind of story television shows might be based on—like *Dallas*, for instance. But the question is, why do we have to do this? Should we put pressure on kids to be in the family business if that's not where their hearts are, if that's not where their passions lie?

Look, a family business is a wonderful rock of stability. I think it's a great option to have if a family is fortunate enough, and I never grew up wanting for anything. It's an awesome opportunity for kids to have that path ahead of them, but I don't think they should be pushed. I think they should be encouraged, if that's what they want.

I would love my kids to follow whatever business I operate, but I do not think it is something that should be mandatory. I believe kids should be given the option to decide for themselves what to do.

At the same time, whether because of family obligations or for other reasons, I think a lot of people are living the life that they think they should live or feel they have to live. People don't stop to reflect. They don't undertake deep introspection into what they are doing or what they really want to do with their life. They don't ask themselves the hard questions.

If I had all the money and time in the world, what would I do?

There's that great question: if I had all the money and time in the world, what would I do? Interesting things come from asking yourself that question. I think a lot of people don't understand why they do the things they do, why they make the choices they make. They think they have to follow a certain path, a career path, or develop a bigger business and compete with everyone based on what they believe others think they should be doing. What they think is important is influenced by the society, the culture they live in, where they are from, how they were raised, and so forth. They have voices in their head, telling them what they can and cannot do. I believe all of us, no matter how independent we think we are, have experienced this at one point or another.

A WAKE-UP CALL

I want to send a wake-up call to people to help them realize they are allowed to stop and think about what kind of life they're living and they have the option to make the changes they want to make. I am not saying it's easy. Of course, I can hear some of you saying, "That's easy for you to say, Jofi, because you had the family business." But I truly believe we all have the option to think about and be aware of the choices we have.

Maybe you make your own choice and realize, "Yes, this is the life I want to have. I know I am sacrificing time I could spend with my family. I know I'm sacrificing time I could have to myself. I know my health might eventually be jeopardized because I'm working too much." But at least you know. You're aware of the kind of life you're living, and you know the pros and cons of that kind of life, rather than living in cruise control mode and not feeling anything. However, I have a feeling that if you paused to think, you would make some changes to the way you are living your life. Awareness makes a difference. So stop and think.

Awareness makes a difference. So stop and think.

That's it, in a nutshell. That's my philosophy behind putting this book together. As you read this book, I want you to hear that message and make it part of your life plan. I want people to make the changes they feel are necessary. I don't want to tell people what they have to do. My only suggestion is that you stop and think about the life you're living now.

You have a purpose. You have a meaning in life.

You have a purpose. You have a meaning in life. Ask yourself: Am I happy? Truly happy? And based on the answer that you come up with, you make decisions about the kinds of changes that you feel are necessary for you to live the kind of life you want to live. Happiness will be at the center of your purpose.

An Integral Coach®

Integral Coaching® programs encompass an ongoing, evolving methodology intended to be the most comprehensive response to human life. Its practitioners reach deeply into the past, gathering wisdom from East and West, while simultaneously staying current with the frontiers of new discoveries in the cognitive science, genetics, and other disciplines.

Source: New Ventures West at www.newventureswest.com.

In my new role as an Integral Coach®, I don't know what the future holds for me. It's not as clear as it was when I was part of the family business. Yet, I still chose this role. I knew I would be happy, and I knew I would do well by following my heart, doing what I wanted to do.

The point is that I decided to follow my passion, which is to help people. I realized that by being a coach, by being a speaker, by writing a book, I can help people. It will allow me to do a lot of good in this world, and that gives me energy. I tell everybody who asks me about my newfound path in life that there are other people who also have a passion and are following it, no matter what. They end up being successful. They're very happy. They are role models for me.

I truly believe that by following my passion, everything is going to fall into place.

Yes, I still have worries. I especially have worries now that I am on my own. Still, the point is that I truly believe that by following my passion, everything is going to fall into place. I'm going to be happy following my passion, and I know that by doing so, I'll make enough money to live. Sometimes people don't realize that. It's very hard for a lot of people, I think, to understand that. They try to rationalize all the decisions they make. People ask me, "Jofi, is this part-time? Is there something else you're doing in the meantime?"

My answer to them always is, "No, this is full-time for me," because for me, coaching is my full-time passion.

People question this, telling me bluntly, "Jofi, you're not going to be successful." I may think, "Wow!" in shock at the negative thoughts they are expressing so openly to me. But I also know they're telling me this because of all those who say there is only one way to be in the business world. I know this isn't true. We can choose our own paths, our own passions.

I keep moving forward because I'm happy doing this. I love being a coach; it is my passion in life. I love helping people. I'm going to be happy doing so, and I know I'm going to be successful. How big, how small my practice will be, I don't know yet. But what I do know is that if I follow the right path for me, everything's going to work out, and I will make a difference in this world.

When reading my book—and, I think, any book—I recommend you read it with an open mind and absorb what I'm saying. Reflect on the words and think about how they relate to your own life, to your own experience. Your experiences won't exactly resemble mine, but much of what I discuss in my book may relate to the emotions you have felt, the experiences you've had in your own life, and the way you think about all of it. If you read this book carefully, I think you'll find a lot of similarities between our experiences that will be meaningful to you.

I received a lot of negative responses from people who heard what I wanted to do in life. One thing I think of when I hear these voices is something the late Steve Jobs, the genius behind Apple, used to say, "Don't let the noise of others' opinions drown out your inner voice." That's what I'm going through right now. In the past, I followed everybody's opinion, and I wouldn't listen to my own inner voice. Now, I'm following my own voice and moving forward, no matter what's happening around me.

Thanks for joining me on this path.

TABLE OF CONTENTS

Join a Journey to Discover "What Do You Want in Life?"

No one ever asked me, "Jofi, what would make you happy?" After we sold the family business, I had an opportunity to think about this. It was the perfect time to wonder about what to do next in my life and my career. In fact, this was the first time I ever asked myself the question: "Jofi, what do you really want in life?"

Once you open yourself up to this question, you might surprise yourself with the path you take— and the answers you find!

On my journey, I realized that I had been living my life on cruise control. I had a "perfect" life, but I didn't feel like I was my own person, living my own life. For example, while working at our insurance organization, I wore a suit and tie every day. But that's not my style! I am more comfortable with a laid-back, casual look. That's what makes me happy. Also, I believe I was a good leader, but I didn't lead my teams in my own way. Instead, I think I copied my father's leadership style, which was fine—but it wasn't *me*.

On my journey, I learned that you are responsible for your own happiness. That you can live a balanced, healthy life. And that you can live a more fulfilling, meaningful life too.

A key discovery was finding what makes me happy.

My path led me to New Ventures West, a comprehensive coaching program that leads to insights and opens up possibilities. Through this intensive program, I discovered two key things that make me really happy: my family and helping others.

My path led me to become certified as an Integral Coach® to guide others to turn off cruise control and discover what makes them happy.

Think about the life YOU are living.

Take a moment to ponder these questions:
- Am I living my life on cruise control?
- What do I really want?
- What makes me happy?
- What small thing can I do, right now, to live a happier, more meaningful life?

I invite you to keep reading! Join me on my journey to become my own person, to live authentically, and to discover what I call "my happy self." Reading this book may be the first step on your path to turn off cruise control, discover what makes you happy, and create a healthy, more meaningful life. Reading this book may be the first step to find "your happy self."

Jofi Baldrich
Coach – Speaker – Author

CHAPTER ONE

Values from My Family Background

My father was very close to his father, my grandfather. One story I remember was that when my dad was seven years old, my grandfather had half of his stomach taken out in an operation at Johns Hopkins Hospital, and he was forced to retire from his job. This sounded like a terrible thing to go through, and it certainly was, but the advantage was he could spend more time with his children and so he learned more about what my father liked to do.

When my father was very young, he was a great baseball player. He played double-A baseball in Puerto Rico. He played mostly second base for a local team for fifteen years, retiring when he turned thirty. He was an excellent player, and my grandfather was always there to see him and support him—always, always, always. I think that influenced my dad a lot and showed him how to raise me to be very close to him. He was always there for me, and I was always there for him. I am his only son among two girls, just as my grandfather had only one son and two girls. And so it is with me: one son and two daughters.

My dad was always my coach in basketball and baseball and, as his father had been there for him, he was always there for me. It's one of those things. When I talk to my childhood friends, we remember that our parents were *always there* at our games, as a coach or as a dad. You don't see the same commitment from the parents today. Instead, parents may say, "We cannot come because we are too busy." I really appreciated my dad's closeness, his being there for us. That is the kind of thing I also want to give to all three of my kids: the gift of always being there for all of their activities. Being there has more value than anything material I can give them.

Being there has more value than anything material I can give them.

My dad and I are very close. We actually look alike, and this was especially true when we were younger. I had an interesting experience one recent Sunday, while I was putting this book together. I was attending mass at church. An elderly gentleman, who knew nothing about me, came up and asked, "Are you the son of Junior Baldrich? You have to be! You have to be, when I saw your son and you."

I said yes, of course. It turns out that he and my father were great friends. I must tell you things like this happen to me a lot when I am out. People see me, my face, and they realize I must be my father's son. When he was younger, my son looked even more like my dad than I do. The family resemblance across generations is very strong.

I look like my dad. What the heck! I'm told this a lot and I'm very proud of it, to tell you the truth.

RETURNING FOR THE FAMILY

I want to tell you a quick story about when I was in college at Mount Saint Mary's College in Emmitsburg, Maryland. I really didn't know what to do with my life at the time. My dad talked to me about going back to Puerto Rico and joining him in the business; he had his own insurance company. During this period of my life, I was playing tennis for my school. I decided to work as a professional tennis teacher for a couple years before going to get my MBA in insurance and finance in New York. After that, I started working full time. I worked almost two years in Miami before going back to Puerto Rico and working with my father.

My father had established an excellent insurance organization. For one of the companies we represented, we were their exclusive managing general agent for Puerto Rico. After a few years of representing them successfully, they decided to cancel our contract and work directly with the clients—no more agents for them. The crazy thing is that most of that company's clients were there because of my father. He was the one who had brought the clients to the company and made it grow. The company management decided that, after all the business he had brought them, they no longer needed him. I worked in Miami for the company. My father called me and said, "I think it's best if you come home now."

The fact of the matter is that my father did not take this setback lying down. He bounced back stronger than ever, moving forward with his own company, without worrying too much. At least, that is the impression he gave me. He was always a very positive person and a heck of a salesman. With his enthusiasm and leadership, the family company kept moving forward. We had a great business. Everything that happened in our business happened for a reason and we could not complain.

Still, at the time, I was worried about what was going to happen. Just think about somebody coming to you and saying, "We're cutting you off. We're going direct to the client, no middle man," and most of your major clients are with that company. I was really worried. I didn't know what was going to happen. I was brand new in the business world. I was scared for my dad, wondering how he was going to react and what would happen to the family business and all our employees. I was happy—surprised really—by the way he reacted. He continued moving forward with the business. There was no time to look back. We decided to take another route and said to ourselves, "Let's move on." And we made a lot of money together, as a family, stronger than ever after the setback.

FAMILY STRENGTH

A lot of my strength comes from my family, the way I was raised. I can tell many stories that are examples of this. Once, when I was young, I played in a tennis tournament and I *lost*. I wasn't supposed to lose. It was when I started to play competitively, and so much was still so very new to me. I was at home in the hallway when my mom came to me and hugged me, crying because she felt so bad. Losing didn't hurt me as much as it seemed to hurt my mom. It's one more piece of evidence that we are a very competitive, and at the same time, a very caring family.

Also, whenever we played a game together, my dad always tried to beat me. But once I started beating my dad in tennis, he never beat me again. My little sister was better than I was at tennis, but I'm not sure if she ever beat my dad. My dad would play fun psychological games with her to make sure she would not beat him. We are very competitive. It's in our genes as a family. I am not complaining, because this competitiveness has given me so much strength as an adult.

Another story concerns an occasion when my father and I were playing a doubles tournament for my dad's fraternity, I believe. I might have been fifteen or sixteen years old. We were playing against two adults. A fight started between my dad and one of the other players who used to be a member of the national basketball team in Puerto Rico. Both were allowing their ego and their temper to take control, and I just wanted to get out of the way. To me it was a simple call, nothing big, nothing worth an argument.

WINNING AND LOSING WITH GRACE

At that time, in all those situations, I didn't realize how intense competition could be. I wasn't aware, I guess, because it was normal in my house to behave in a very competitive, challenging manner. As I grew up and became more aware of the kind of life I had been living, I started thinking, "Why do we compete? Why do we have to always do something better than someone else? Why do we always have to be jealous when somebody tells us about what they own, or that their son or daughter did this or that, and so forth? Why can't we simply be happy for them?"

I didn't realize how intense competition could be.

I'm more for enjoying what I have and what I excel in than for being competitive about it. I don't want to say I don't love winning.

I certainly do. The difference is that, now, I look at competitiveness from another point of view. It makes me think of a story my grandfather used to tell us that was based on an old Spanish proverb: Every time you're going someplace, you have to have two bags, one for winning and one for losing. Somebody always has to win, and somebody has to lose, but we can be prepared for that inevitability. Play the best you can, fairly, and be ready. But to be a good winner, you must also prepare to be a good loser. Some people use the phrase "never be a sore loser." It's the same concept: be gracious under the pressure of competition. Moreover, be gracious if it turns out that, even after trying your best, you lose.

My grandfather's view and my view at the time might have conflicted a little, but the older I get, the easier it is to understand his viewpoint. Maybe in the past I would have been upset about losing. I would have asked myself why: "Why did it have to be like that? Why couldn't I just *win*?" Now I know a better thing to tell myself: "Try to win, but if you don't, move forward."

WHEN COMPETITION OVERWHELMS YOU

Life is much more than simply a game to be won or lost. It is so much richer when you choose to be happy and understand competition is only one aspect of life. When you see athletes retiring early, making changes in their lives after a great career, many of them will say, "Well, life is not just about tennis"—or basketball, or whatever sport. "Life is much more than that. This is one part of my life, and it's over, and I'm going to move forward with my life." This is refreshing to hear, because I have found a lot of people become engulfed by just one thing, and they don't become involved in the rest of their lives, in other aspects of living. That's what being too immersed in competition can do to you. What we need to do sometimes is step back and ask ourselves how we are letting our competitiveness and the desire to win overtake our lives.

Life is much more than simply a game to be won or lost.

I think being competitive always makes you work harder, which can be a good thing, but you have to be careful it doesn't work to your detriment, that it doesn't damage relationships, the way you see things and people around you. For instance, you may not be happy the rest of the day, because you lost a game. You may even think the whole week is over for you. Instead, you should accept that you lost the game—or a big business deal. Even though you gave it your best effort, it just didn't work out. And you should tell yourself to move forward. Learn from your experience but move forward. This is my philosophy now. This is how I have come to see things.

Learn from your experience but move forward.

My father and his father, everyone in my family for that matter, taught me to be competitive. The good of that upbringing is that I always aim to be successful. The disadvantage is that it can be detrimental if I focus too much on being competitive and let that focus overtake other components of my life. Don't let your competitiveness bring out your bad side because you want to win so much you lose control. Be aware of that. Don't let your competitiveness eat you up inside.

Don't let your competitiveness eat you up inside.

For me, it's been up and down because of the insecurity I have felt until recently about what's going to happen in my future. It has taken me a while to realize this is my path, this is what I want to do. The more time that passes, the more I'm convinced I chose the right path for me. I firmly believe everything happens at the right time, at the right moment. Some people are faster. Some people are slower. Some people take more time to make decisions. Others make decisions more quickly. Everybody has his or her own timing. Everything happens for a reason. For me, it has always worked that way.

This book was something I wanted to write almost three years ago, and it didn't happen. Finally, I made the decision that it was going to happen, and here it is; it has happened. I realize that over the years there were many things I wanted to do, related to what I'm doing now. Instead, I doubted myself. I listened to the negative voices. Now, I'm coming back, and I'm doing those things because I'm absolutely convinced they are what I need to do, and I am moving forward with them.

Taking this initiative is not the same as making a business plan in which you know exactly the steps you will take. I know my end goal, but I'm not sure of what will happen before that. I'm going to write a book. I'm going to speak. I'm going to do coaching, group coaching, one-on-one. We'll see how it develops. How I share my passion to help others is still to be decided. It's an ongoing project. It changes even as it develops. Maybe just writing this book is the answer, or speaking, or doing both, or just coaching one-on-one, or group coaching, maybe a little bit of everything. If I don't try, I will never know, though, and this is the path that I find myself on right now. I am following my passions, the greatest of which is to help others, and I will see where all of this leads me.

I am following my passions, the greatest of which is to help others, and I will see where all of this leads me.

I'm following the values instilled in me as a youth and finding balance in my life at the same time. Based on everything my mom and my dad taught me while growing up, and on my experience, I find there's much more than balance involved. After all, I think it would be very hard to find exact balance in *everything* you want to do. The question becomes, then, how you integrate everything you need to do in your life based on your values and not get lost along the way. How do you become a role model for others? I think it takes an acrobat's equilibrium, the ability to continually correct yourself to avoid falling over.

I'll give you a great example of what I'm doing. I'm going to be away from my home soon for an extended period—a business trip. That means being away from my wife and my three kids. I cannot tell you enough how deeply I miss them every time I leave, but I am following my passion. This is what I love to do. This is what makes me happy. This is what motivates me. This is what brings sparkle into my eyes.

Still, I make sure that I can integrate all of this when I am at work. There are times when I am going to say no. When I realize I'm traveling too much, I'll have to make my trips shorter, do whatever I have to quickly, and come back to my family.

Sometimes when I'm home, I'm aware that I don't want my personal or professional activities to reduce the time I spend with my kids. I'm going to plan my whole day so I can take care of myself.

So let's say working hours are during the day when the kids are at school. If I want to go to the gym for a workout, I am not going to do that during my family time in the evening. Instead, I'll probably pick up my girls at dance class or my son at basketball. I feel much better when I try to balance my love for my family and my passion for my work and personal activities.

At the same time, my son, who's the youngest, at nine years old, is fully aware of when my business travel commitments take my attention away from his needs. I feel bad each time he asks, "Dad, are you going to be at this?" and he mentions an event from school or another activity he wants me to attend with him. He already knows the answer might be no. He realizes I travel a lot. I might tell him, "Yes, as of right now, I'll be there. So, yes, I can take you to this place." It's tough sometimes. Why does my son have to ask if I'm going to be home so that we can go to a place together?

The way I look at it is I'm following my passion. I'm doing what I love to do, and I think that it makes me a better father. It makes me a better family man. It helps me in the other arenas of my life when I follow my passion. It is better for all of those around me, in business, in friendships, and especially in my family, when I follow my passions and live out my dreams.

I'm doing what I love to do,
and I think that it makes me a better father.

CHAPTER TWO

Following Your Passions and Dreams

There are many anecdotes I can tell you about following dreams. They include what happened to me when we sold the family insurance business, and I had more time to catch up with longtime friends and business contacts over lunch. Virtually every one of them told me what they thought my next step in life should be, what they thought my new business plan should be. I know deep inside they always had my best interests at heart, even if, quite often, their ideas were not what I wanted to do with my life and had nothing to do with my passions.

For example, at lunch, a friend might say something like, "Jofi, you should get in the business of selling red chairs because nobody is selling red chairs in Puerto Rico and you can make a lot of money. It is something I have analyzed and I would do it, but I have my business. At the moment, because you are doing nothing, it's perfect for you." I had conversations like that for a while, but the problem was that nobody asked me what my passion was, what it was I loved to do. No one asked me what I wanted my next step in life to be. When they gave me advice, my friends never considered who the real me was.

Nobody ever asked me what would make me happy.

Nobody ever asked me what would make me happy.

Of course, even following our passions, we can be led astray, not seeing the forest for the trees.

In helping people understand this, I have always used the example of opening a restaurant. Let's imagine I want to open a restaurant because I believe it is something that could make me a lot of money. My thoughts would be as follows:

Okay, Jofi, so here we are. Let's open a restaurant because we know we can make a lot of money with it. First, we need a location. Are we renting or owning that place? I am not sure. Let's move on to the next issue. Now we have to hire the employees, and having employees could be trouble. For a restaurant, I would need as many as fifty employees. Then the food. We have to be very careful when buying food, because it could become rotten —spoilage is expensive and we would lose money. And then I would have to work almost every day, morning, noon, and night, until very late. Why so late? Because I will be open for dinner. This will have the greatest impact on my family as I will get home late and my family will be none too happy about that. And don't forget about selling liquor in the restaurant. I need to get a license, maybe go up against a community board that does not want another venue selling alcohol in the neighborhood. If I overcome that obstacle, I will have to deal with people who might get drunk in the restaurant.

And it goes on and on like that. In the end, what do I tell myself? "All of this is a deal killer. Forget about opening a restaurant. It is simply too hard."

What happened? I was thinking about the business just to make money, not about what motivated me, what my passion was, what moved me. This is what happened. I took the wrong approach to this issue and it did not work.

In my current coaching work, I am following my passion. All of those same problems and situations might still arise. I deal with them, however, because they are not going to stop me from doing what I want to do. Many of the people around me still tell me I'm not going to be successful, or that in Puerto Rico nobody knows what coaching is or how to hire a coach. If they do know anything about coaching, they will bring hotshot coaches from around the world to their businesses rather than use local talent. "They bring those kinds of guys over, not you, Jofi" is something I often hear from people around me. People throw all kinds of thoughts at me, including one I mentioned earlier in the book, "Jofi, aren't you going to do this part-time?" Many people don't believe my passion can be full-time.

I believe many people are afraid of what they don't know. Such people don't realize that instead of pointing out their own fears and insecurities when I talk about my passion, they should instead ask me, "Why do you do what you do, Jofi? What is it that moves you to do this kind of work?" This is the question we should all be asking ourselves: Why do we do what we do?

This is the question we should all be asking ourselves: Why do we do what we do?

41

That's a great question I wish people asked me more often. Why do you do what you do? I coach because it is my passion. I am energized by it. I love helping people. As I write this book, I am in the middle of a course I am taking for a certificate in positive psychology, CIPP, with Professor Tal Ben-Shahar, Ph.D. One of the reflective questions that I recently answered during class was about how to bring more flow into your life, much like being "in the zone" in sports lingo, where everything you're doing works perfectly. It is a feeling of ultimate concentration, a feeling that nothing can go wrong. When I realized this, I understood I needed to make some changes in my life, including improving my schedule to be more productive.

I love talking to friends and helping them out when they need my help. Yet, this is not ideal if I do it during the peak hours of my own business. The argument is not that I do not want to do it, as I love helping my friends. It is that I must not do it at times when I should focus on work for my clients and other aspects of my business. I still, of course, like to make time for friends and their issues. I just schedule that time during the afternoon, when I would not normally be as productive working for my paying clients. Friends share their expertise with friends who need help. Do you get paid to do that? No, of course not. But if your friends rely on you, you take the call. You give them advice for half an hour. You help them out. It is what friends do. It is not that we measure these things out, but we know that in our own time of need our friends will do the same for us.

My optimum work rhythm is in the morning. If I work from 8:00 a.m. to 1:00 p.m. with as few interruptions as possible, I know I can be at my most productive, dealing with aspects of my business that require the most concentration. Within this time frame, I can achieve what most people can within a typical eight-hour day. My belief is that everyone should find his or her most productive hours, when the work rhythm simply flows. Once you find what works best for you, use that knowledge to your advantage. I can tell you from experience that there is a huge difference between finding your flow versus not finding it. I find the afternoon works best for the minor things in my coaching business, things that are done in short bursts, that don't require intense thoughtfulness and planning. That is when I take care of things such as answering e-mails, returning phone calls, writing short notes. Knowing when you are the most productive, whether it is the morning or the evening, or even 3:00 a.m. when the rest of the world is sleeping, can help reduce stress too. We do not all have to be nine-to-five people, working within the time constraints others dictate to us.

REFLECTING ON YOUR LIFE

We must all give ourselves permission to be human.

Each of us has to find that flow, that time, and that pattern that allows us to work most efficiently. I think that's the tough part for a lot of people. One of the key ideals I have learned in my positive psychology course is that we must all give ourselves permission to be human. You are going to make mistakes. Things are going to happen. There is no right or wrong way to do something. Instead, we must simply take that first step. Go ahead and do it and learn for yourself, learn from those mistakes. People are used to the quick answer, the quick solution. Many people simply want to go online, get on the Internet and find the answer, but life doesn't work like that. There's no magic pill to be happy or to find meaning in your life, to find purpose, to find your passion. You have to work at it. You can, of course, get help. There are people who can coach and guide you and give you advice as you make your decisions. In the end, however, the one who's going to find the answer and make the decision is you. No one else. You can ask a lot of people their opinion about what you should do, but in the end, the most important thing is to learn from their experiences and apply them to your own. You have to do what's best for you, not for anybody else. At the end of the day, who's going to be there, doing whatever it is that you decided to do? You. Not the other people. It is you who must live with these decisions.

> ## *You have to do what's best for you, not for anybody else.*

Sometimes it's difficult when everybody is against an idea or people simply do not understand. Once I was having drinks at a party and a friend came up and said, "Jofi, what are you doing now that you've sold your business?" I told my friend about my coaching, and he replied, "What the heck is a coach? What kind of coaching do you do?" I'm thinking, "I had one drink. I don't know how many drinks he had. It's loud. It's noisy, music, everybody dancing, having a great time. Do I really want to go deep and answer this question now? Does he really want to listen?"

At the beginning, I had doubts about talking about coaching for many reasons, including those I just listed. Now I just tell everybody. Period. This is what I do. My passion is to help people, young and old, find happiness and meaning in their life. I find I can help many people who are young to make a decision right off the bat. When you're older, I help you regroup, rediscover what you want, and make a change in your life if that's what you're looking for.

I am very happy with the decision I have made to be a coach. I do not know where it will take me exactly, but I know I will be happy doing this, and I will be making a difference in this world. I will continue moving forward and learning from my mistakes along the way.

DOING WHAT MAKES YOU HAPPY
WITH OTHERS' NEEDS IN MIND

One of my other points, though, is that while I'm doing what makes me happy, I also try to make sure my wife and family do not feel left out. I involve them in many of my decisions because I know that my decisions affect them too. This way, I can make decisions for myself in harmony with the needs of my family. We'll talk more about this topic in the next chapter. While we've talked a lot about doing things that make you happy, doing the things that you want to do, and listening to your inner voice, part of the balance in the real world involves keeping your family—or, if you do not have a family, the other important people in your life—involved in your decisions. So this is sort of shifting gears, but I think that while we are still pursuing what we want to do, having constant communication with other family members and the important people in our life helps us integrate all that we really care about.

One of the things I'm doing now in my new role as an Integral Coach® is talking to my wife to make sure that she's okay with all my travel. For example, I had a job in Maui, Hawaii—certainly not a bad place to work—and I was gone for nine days. I came home for about a week, and then I left to take a course, which meant even more time away from my wife and my children. Before signing up for my course, I talked to my wife. "Listen, I have this great opportunity to take this course. It lasts ten months and I get two sessions with the professor in person. One is in August. One is in April. This is what's going to happen." By involving her in the decision-making process, I knew that she would be fine with it, and I went ahead and registered for the class.

My wife also knows I would have said no if she had not wanted me to go away again. I want to make sure she approves by getting her involved in the decision making. She knows how much I value her opinion. She's always been very supportive of everything I do. She rarely says no. I cannot think of a single time when she said no to any aspect of my being an Integral Coach®. At the same time that I'm learning all this for my job, it helps me as a person, as a husband, as a father, as a friend, because I'm continually becoming a better person, a more understanding, loving, caring, open person. Coaching is about personal growth, and it spreads to the other arenas of my life, as a father, husband, son, brother, and uncle, and in the many other roles I play.

Actually, from my viewpoint, it looks as if everybody wins. I think my wife will laugh when she reads this book because I mention her so much. In the course I am taking, there is a big sheet of paper on which everyone in the class writes his or her goal for the next year. My goal is to wake up in a happy mood each day. Normally I'm a grouch in the morning. My wife jokes that she can only ask me yes or no questions when I wake up.

I can't go into a deep conversation about the meaning of life at 6:00 a.m. in the morning. I want to wake up happy. My wife is a happy morning person. We wake up together close to 5:00 a.m. every day. I want to do that in a good mood rather than my usual grouchy one. I know this change is not going to happen in a day. It's going to be a process. Indeed, I'm already seeing results, but I know this change will take a long time to accomplish and become permanent. It is part of everything that I've been going through. All of the learning, coaching, teaching, and the introspection I always do every time I do this kind of work helps me accomplish the goals I have created for myself. It's a process that we all can undertake.

CHAPTER THREE

Integrate Your Work with Life:
Be Aware of the Balance or Lack of It

We have to be aware of our time, how we spend our time, how we divide our time. Most of all, we have to look at how that impacts our family and those who are important to us. The irony is that many times what I hear from people about why they work so hard and stay at the office late at night are excuses. They use their family to justify their behavior. They say things like, "I do this for them. That's why I have to work late or go into the office on weekends."

I believe the only thing kids want, especially when they are growing up, is time with their mom and dad. They really don't want a bigger house or whatever it is their parents are working so hard for. They just want time with their parents, and I think it's extremely important we provide them that time. Very often, when we are focused on material needs and work for them, we forget about the emotional needs of those we love.

Very often, when we are focused on material needs and work for them, we forget about the emotional needs of those we love.

It's often very sad to see successful people and their relationship with their kids. Often, that relationship is nowhere to be found because they have concentrated their life on their business, not their children and the home they should be building for them. Many people have forgotten those they are doing all the hard work for, and that, I believe, is the key. How do you accomplish everything you want to do in your life and make it happen? Sometimes you're going to have to say no to certain things, and you have to realize what's important in your life. Sometimes we take on too many things, and sometimes we feel we have to say yes to a lot of people who ask for our help, no matter what it is—a charity, for example. All that ends up costing you in terms of your health or your relationship with your family. Even if you're doing good because you're helping a charity or somebody in need, in the end, you have to think of yourself and be aware of what's important to you. In the order of importance, how do you divide your time: friends, work, family? Are you overcommitted, ignoring those who are the most important to you, trying to please others instead?

You think you spend a lot of time with your family, but when you see how much actual time you're spending doing other things, you'll be surprised. I see parents taking their son or daughter by the hand as they go from the parking lot to the classroom, and the majority of the time they're looking at the BlackBerry or the iPhone for updates from work, or the latest stock price. Is that really spending time with your son? Is that really being there with your daughter when you take her to school?

Be present when you're with your family.

Be present when you're with your family. Enjoy them. We wonder why it sometimes takes something big or bad to happen before we appreciate what we have. You have to be aware when you're spending time with your loved ones that you must really be there for them, emotionally and physically.

For me, for example, it's very hard, now, with my teenage girls, but with my son it's different. With my son it might just be whatever he wants to do. We watch TV together, assemble Legos, go to the pool, and so forth. With my daughters, the situation is different. I have to make accommodations to be there for them when they need me and when they're ready to talk or hang out with their dad—that kind of thing. With daughters, I find it cannot be on my time. I've got to be flexible. I have to go with the flow. You shouldn't be expecting to control everything, especially when family demands your time.

For example, I know I travel a lot and in the near future that aspect of my work will only increase, taking more of my time away from my family. I believe that I have to be conscious of that when I'm home and make sure to maximize the time I spend with them. It's kind of a feeling that I have to make up for the time I am away.

I realized I needed to be cognizant of my time away from my family when I was training for a triathlon for over a year and a half. Every Monday, Wednesday, and Friday at 5:00 a.m. I was religiously at the swimming pool. I woke up each of those days as early as 4:00 a.m. That meant I had to go to bed at 9:00 p.m., at the latest by 10:00 p.m. This tremendous time commitment and grueling physical regimen meant that by 7:00 p.m., during what should have been my ideal family time, I was already moody and grouchy at home. You have to go running. You have to hit the bicycle—all the stuff to make you healthy and strong for the triathlon. Still, I realized my athletic training was taking away time from my family and hurting my relationship with them, even when I tried to make time for them.

FAMILY TIME

In that respect, I am evaluating my athletic life right now to decide my priorities. I got caught up in the popular wave of triathlons in Puerto Rico. It's kind of like a drug. You're exercising and it's good from that point of view, but when you take it to the extreme, it hurts the other arenas of your life you should also be focusing on. Now I'm trying to decide what to do. Do I want to go running? Do I want to go swimming? When is the best time for me to do those things? To avoid hurting my relationship with my wife and kids, I must exercise and prepare during school hours—basically, during business hours. This is another aspect of balance, and it is important to consider as I manage my sacred family time.

For example, a typical work day has so many inputs and outputs. This afternoon, after using my daytime "work time" putting this book together, I'll be helping my wife because everything came together, doctor appointments and extracurricualar activities with the kids. How will I do this? In the morning, I woke up early and I worked out for an hour to prepare for the triathlon. I also worked on the book for about forty-five minutes while my kids were sleeping, again limiting the time I take away from them.

When I am with my family, knowing I have been able to get work done helps me feel that I have more quality time. I feel it's about just being there. It's not that anything important is happening this afternoon or tonight, just hanging out with my kids, just being in the house with them and going to their room, asking them what kind of test they have, talking to them, being involved with them, knowing their friends' names.

And on that subject, for all you parents out there reading this book, knowing your children's friends' names is important too. When we were little, in the days before cell phones, our friends would call our mother on the house phone. "Hey, Mrs. Baldrich, it's Maria," or "it's Vanessa" or "it's John" or "it's Eduardo" or whatever was the name of my friend from school. When we were young, parents knew whom their children were talking to. Now, kids talk on their cell phones so you really don't know whom they're talking to or whom they are interacting with on the Internet, or whatever tools kids are using today to communicate with each other. You have to be really involved in your children's lives to know what's happening and for them to know that you're there for them no matter what. One way that we try to accomplish this is to always eat together, as a family. It's part of our family plan.

Little things count when it's about quality time with our children.

And remember, little things count when it's about quality time with our children. I believe a lot of people forget about the importance of simply spending time with their children, and it doesn't really matter what you do. I think some people get hung up on "We've got to go to Disney World," or "We've got to do something exciting with them. We've got to do something big," when it's really just about the time itself, making sure it's quality time, not focusing on how much money you have spent while you're with them. It's really just about being there and spending time with them. All that children want is time.

When I talk to people who go on different types of vacations, I just love it: taking an RV for a couple of weeks, the whole family, or maybe it's two or three RVs with different friends and their families; going camping; going hiking; just getting away. Two years ago we spent six weeks in Boulder, Colorado, as a family, just the five of us; it was the best experience ever. Part of the time we rented a house in the mountains. The kids went to day camp. We did different things during the week. There were horses, and a dog. We went hiking. We went on a balloon ride. We went water rafting, and cycling. We did all kinds of adventurous things. We were outdoors most of the time, barely ever on the Internet, barely anything electronic around us. That made it the best time we ever had as a family. We didn't have to buy any new clothes or any new shoes or any new make-up or go to Disney or anything else like that. We were simply being together, just the five of us. I did not even want my own parents along, as much as they love their grandchildren. I told them, almost jokingly, "No. You cannot go. It's just a time for us five. That's it. No visitors, period." It was a fantastic experience to have shared with the family, and I am looking forward to doing it again. Yes, of course, I did have to spend money on the trip, but it wasn't about the amount of money, like some glamour vacations I hear about from my friends. Instead it was about a vacation created in such a way that what the money bought was more time with my wife and kids without distractions from our family's togetherness.

For us, as a family, it was about just having a great time together, just being there. Even when you're home on what's called a staycation, you can do that, or even on vacation at the homes of other members of the family.

For example, my wife is from Panama and we go there for Thanksgiving week. We joke because I'm a planner and my wife is not. When we are there on weekdays, everybody's working. So what do I do? I get bored sometimes because I cannot be around the people we came to visit. It's part of my sacrifice when I take my wife to see her entire family. The kids are going to have a great time, and I'll do my part to make the best of it. I could complain and some might say I have a right to do so and win the case against visiting, if you want to put it that way. But it's not about winning or losing. It's about family. It's about being with your loved ones and this is the time for my wife to be with her family and for me to make my bond with them stronger, not to mention my kids getting time with all their cousins and aunts and uncles. It's part of balancing everything you do in your life when you are married, a sacrifice that is not really a sacrifice but a way to get closer to the relatives of the one you love.

INVOLVING FAMILY IN DECISIONS

Despite my wife's and my jokes about self-sacrifice and taking turns with our families, a serious issue is involved that I want to talk about in this chapter. It's important to involve the family in your decisions.

It's important to involve the family in your decisions.

I'll give you a great example. I always wanted to live away from Puerto Rico for a year or two so the family can experience everything that would come from that. Perhaps I should have done it after we sold the business, but I didn't. Almost two years ago, my desire to leave Puerto Rico grew stronger, and we started talking about it as a family.

My wife was okay with it. One of my daughters was okay with it. My other daughter said no, and my son started crying. Still, to further the decision-making process, we talked about it. In the end, we didn't do it. Also, because I traveled so much, it wouldn't have been fair to leave my wife alone in whatever new place we had moved to, without friends and family who would be there for an emergency, or simply be with my wife if she were lonely. So we stayed in Puerto Rico.

Now, when we have these discussions, we think about the kinds of vacations we can go on together as a family, just the five of us. It's what I was saying before: I could have made the decision as the father and head of the household, or as the breadwinner, and made them go wherever I chose. I could have been dictatorial as some fathers— even parents—might be, without input from my children. That way, though, maybe no one would have had a great time. When I related this experience, friends told me, "Jofi, you should have done it, period, end of discussion with your family." I don't think they were right. It's kind of like leading by example, modeling the behavior you want them to learn. I think it worked out for the best. Things happen for a reason. Instead of moving away, for example, we just moved to a new house, and that has been our big adventure. Everybody's very happy. And all of these decisions we made together as a family.

THE GREAT RAT RACE

One thing I have also learned from looking at my life and considering the importance of family is that no matter how fast we run, we always lose in the rat race. You think you'll be happy at the next level, but once you achieve that next step, you look for something bigger. You're never finished with the rat race, and it can easily consume your time, your self-esteem, your love of the things you do, the things that make you who you actually are.

No matter how fast we run, we always lose in the rat race.

Research has already proved that any time you achieve something in the rat race, the happy feeling of reaching your goal is just momentary.

From the book Happier, *by Tal Ben-Shahar, Ph.D., the term rat race refers to those who are always doing something today for a future benefit, never enjoying the present, assuming once they reach their next goal, they will find happiness.*

During a study, professors at schools such as Harvard were asked how they felt once they had received tenure and lost their fear of being fired at any time. The great majority felt they would be happier with tenure at their university.

The researchers went back later to revisit the professors who had received tenure. Yes, these professors were happier after they received it, but after a few months, they went back to the same level of happiness as before. The same thing happened to those who did not receive tenure. At first they were not happy, but after some time, they went back to the same level of happiness they had before. The study findings basically tell you it's not about reaching the next milestone or level. It's about trying to find what makes you happy, what gives meaning to your life.

It's about trying to find what makes you happy, what gives meaning to your life.

People get confused about the corner office, becoming the manager, becoming the supervisor, and so forth. There's a great story about someone who starts at the very lowest entry level—such as the mail room—in a publishing house, and then he becomes a copywriter, then assistant editor, and then editor. He is always looking for the next thing to further his position in the company, the next mark of achievement. He spends his whole life there. He becomes editor, senior editor, president, chairman, until it is time to retire and leave space for the next person. His whole life has been focused on achieving the next level and that is it. He never actually enjoys his life because achieving corporate status isn't what really makes you happy. You don't have time to experience the rest of your life, the other arenas of your life that you should be enjoying. Instead, you are always worried about, always focused on, the next step, because that's what you feel is best. That's why it's very refreshing for me to see people make decisions based on what makes them happier, not on making the most money or gaining the most prestige.

Another story tells of a professor whose student comes to him for advice. "I have two job offers, including one I don't like, but it makes the most money and it will help my career path. The other pays less, but it's what I love to do, though it's not going to help the career path I'd like for myself. What should I do?" Her professor tells her, "Make the decision that makes you happy today and in the future."

Only you can make decisions about your life, no one else.

Here's one more thing I want to leave you with before we move ahead.

A huge number of people experience declining health when they retire, while other retirees gain improved health and become happier. Why is that? Those people who become sadder and unhealthier are people whose only purpose in life is to work. Once they stop working, they realize there's nothing out there for them and they get lost. The retirees who thrive seem to have found passion in their life. They have found something that really makes them happy, and they continue with their life. I think, sadly, there are many people in the group for whom life is all about work. Don't get me wrong. We have to work. We have to make a living, bring home the bacon, support our families and ourselves, but there's much more to life than work.

I was just reading an article the other day about all the recent medical graduates becoming doctors, but it's not anymore about working twenty-four- to thirty-six-hour shifts because you're a doctor and you have to. It's also about finding a balance in your life, how you integrate everything while being a doctor. People are more aware that it's not solely about a career path. It's not just about a rat race but also about leading the life you want. We are seeing these goals expressed in this new generation.

Ironic, isn't it, that it's the young people who are teaching us about finding the balance in our lives? Yet, again, there is always something to learn from everyone around us. It's a matter of taking the time to listen, to learn, and to find the ability to live the life you want to live.

It's a matter of taking the time to listen, to learn, and to find the ability to live the life you want to live.

CHAPTER FOUR

What Kind of Life
Are You Living?

After we sold the family business, I certainly had a lot more time on my hands. This meant I found myself in search of what to do next. I started exercising more, did a few marathons, a couple of triathlons, learned scuba diving, and became a Divemaster.

As I looked back at the life I had been living while I was working in the family business, I realized I was living on what I like to call cruise control. I was going through life, basically, doing what I thought I was supposed to be doing. People do this in many ways and at many points in their lives.

Looking back, I feel I was doing everything because it was meant to be or supposed to be, according to what other people around me thought, according to their expectations and those of society. Sometimes, because of this, you just go on autopilot, unaware of the life you are living. After we sold the business, when I had time on my hands and little direction, I started to become introspective about the kind of life I wanted to live from then on, what kind of career choice I wanted to make. I discovered this on my own. I realized I needed to be more aware of the life I was living to make sure I was living the life that I wanted to live and not the life others imposed on me or the life my culture or society expected of me. I refused to listen to people who told me how I should be, according to their expectations, not mine.

That's the process that I'm going through as we sit together here with this book, and that I'll continue to go through for the rest of my life, because, since then, I've been asking myself new questions. I think that at any point in your life you should ask yourself, "What kind of life am I living? Is it the life that I want to live?"

> **"What kind of life am I living?
> Is it the life that I want to live?"**

When you do that and you begin to know yourself better, you can make the changes you feel you need to make. No one else but you should be making decisions about the kind of life you want to live.

That's a little bit about it. The deeper thing is that if you're happy and enjoying your life, people just take it for granted. "Yeah, fine, I'm happy." Yet, if they think more deeply and start reflecting on the life they are living when are they happy and when are they not happy, they might find out they could be even happier. They could be doing things that they would love to be doing. I find instead, maybe even unconsciously, there are people who feel they have no way out of the life they are living if it is a bad one. Others feel that, even if they are unhappy, their miserable life is what they are supposed to be living and there's no other way to live, nothing that can make it better.

People get lost in their own lives when it should not be that way. We should be asking the questions that give us the direction we need to take, the questions that help us find the right way. The answers are not what someone else wants you to do or thinks you should do but what you want to do.

The answers are not what someone else wants you to do or thinks you should do but what you want to do.

I think once you start asking the right questions about the kind of life you want to live, the kind of life you are living, you start getting answers. And those answers are all going to come from within you. You can't find them on the Internet or in a book. Well, all that can help you, or we wouldn't be here together, right now, learning from each other. Still, at the end of the day, you are the one who must make the decision on what kind of life to live and how to live it.

ARE YOU TRULY HAPPY?

Normally when you say hello to people and you ask them if they are happy, they answer, "Yes, yes, I am," almost automatically, almost out of habit, almost mindlessly. But when you are in a setting where people are really talking to each other, maybe a retreat where people open up, you realize that they are not happy, that a lot of them are living lives they think they cannot do anything about. They believe that's the way it's going to be forever, that they are trapped by circumstances.

Instead, what they could be doing is really looking into their lives and figuring out, learning, asking questions about how to get out of it all, to restart their lives again.

Professor Tal Ben-Shahar, Ph.D. in his book *Happier*, talks about four archetypes that describe different patterns of attitude and behaviors. One of them is the rat racer. The rat racer basically thinks that reaching the next goal, the next accomplishment, is what will make him happy. Let's say you realize you're a rat racer: you are always looking for the next opportunity in your job; that's the only goal in your life. But one day you might realize you want to be more balanced and spend more time with your wife or your kids, but you don't know how to do it. There are, however, ways to get help: maybe get a coach, maybe start reading self-help books to help you get out of the rat-race mode and put you on your way to happiness.

I believe sometimes people are afraid of finding out how to make that change.

I believe sometimes people are afraid of finding out how to make that change. They are afraid of finding out what doesn't really make them happy. Change in itself, even from an unhappy state to a happier one, is frightening to many people. So they won't do it. They are afraid to do it. Human beings are not accustomed to change. If you have been living a certain way for the last forty years and then you want to make a change, it's not easy. But it can be done. You've got to just go do it step by step. It's just going to take time, but in the end you are going to be much happier than today.

If you just want to hide behind that curtain of "yes, this is the life I'm supposed to live," or "whatever, I'm stuck here," *you* are making that decision; *you* are making that choice, no one else. Even choosing not to change is a choice.

Even choosing not to change is a choice.

PERSONAL ISSUES WITH THE FAMILY

Looking inside myself has helped me to continue learning about myself, why I do the things I do. It helps me when I speak about it with my family and share with them the things I am learning, what my true passions are. I want them to know what I am doing, why I am doing it, why I am traveling, all the things I feel so passionately about. They get a sense of what it is that I do. My son will sometimes tell me I have the worst job in the world because to him it seems all I do is talk on the phone. That is what he feels, especially when I have a phone call at night in the house. He is too young to know the efforts I went through to get to the point where I can be home at that time, taking that phone call, and still be near him. Of course, ideally, it would be better not to have to take that phone call, but my circumstances are better now. In the past, I would have been making that phone call in the office late at night, nowhere near my family.

Family bonding is strengthened when my wife and kids understand what I do and the difference that I make in other people's lives as a coach. They know if I'm away doing this work that I'm helping other people find their happiness, find meaning in their lives, find their values—whatever it is I'm working on with a particular individual. When my family understands what I do, they become more involved in what I do. It gives them satisfaction to know what I'm doing and why am I doing it. Involving them in my work, in terms of letting them know its importance as well as how much I love doing it, helps the unity of my family.

Involving them in my work, in terms of letting them know its importance as well as how much I love doing it, helps the unity of my family.

I will give you an example from a time I was traveling and working in Singapore. My son wondered why I had to go away, and he was crying about the fact that I was leaving him again.

This experience became part of my work at a Young Presidents' Organization (YPO) workshop I facilitated in Singapore. At the end of the workshop, I organized a circle with everyone in the room, everybody shoulder to shoulder. We numbered 125 people, more or less. I told them about my son's sadness because I was away from home, and I realized tears were flowing down my face. I told them I knew why I was there. It was because I loved my family as much as they did theirs, and by sharing this love with all of them, we could together increase happiness in YPO families around the world. It was my duty, my calling, my passion to be there and share my wealth of knowledge with as many people as I could.

REFRESHING YOUR THOUGHTS ON LIFE

I believe it is important to look at how we live our lives, why we do what we do, and where we want to go. If we do not stop and reflect on our lives, we might end up wondering how we got where we are. By doing this check-up on ourselves, we get a temperature reading of where we are and any changes we feel we need to make in order to follow the path we want to take.

You should make constant reassessments of your life to increase your happiness.

You should make constant reassessments of your life to increase your happiness. It's kind of like getting together at least once a year with your spouse and your kids, or with yourself, or with your partner to think about what you are trying to achieve with your life, your goals, and your happiness. What kind of life are you living? What is it that you want to do? Some people talk about their bucket list, the things they want to do before they kick the bucket—in other words, before they are gone from this earth. Call it whatever you want to call it, but why are you here on this earth? What is your calling? What is your passion? Are you doing what you are most passionate about? You should ask yourself that kind of question, delving deep to find your passion and what you really love to do.

Again, I just think people go on cruise control. For example, they tell themselves they just want to live this life and that's it. For them, there's nothing wrong with that. They are not hurting anybody; they are just living.

Then again, are you really aware of the life that you are living? Do you really understand it? Are you sure that's the kind of life that you really and truly want to live?

ALL THE TIME AND MONEY IN THE WORLD

Sometimes we ask this question, "If you had all the money and all the time in the world, and you could do whatever you wanted, what would you do?" People start thinking about it. They may express ridiculous stuff, goals that are perhaps a little too far-fetched, but, most of the time, they mention things that they can actually do. All their lives they have blocked themselves, thinking many of their goals were not achievable. It can be something simple, say, a weekend trip. They may express a desire to go to Nepal for two weeks to meditate on a mountaintop, or perhaps they always wanted to scuba dive on Australia's Great Barrier Reef. If you have never asked yourself those questions, and you continue living your life on cruise control, convincing yourself everything's good, you will continue on cruise control until the end of your life. Then, when you realize—whoa! Where did all the time go? How did I get here? It might be too late.

That's why I think sometimes when you are talking to people and you see all they have done, it really opens up your eyes. Then you think about what kind of life you are living. Some people go ahead and do something with their lives, and some people just go back to their normal selves the next day.

I recently went on a trip to Cambodia. I don't think, in my old life, the one with the family insurance company, I would have gone there. But I always wanted to. I wanted to find a way to see the ancient monuments, to meditate, to be in a place vastly different from the one where I grew up. But now that I have been there, I often look at the picture of myself that I took with my Blackberry when I was there, and I think of how far along I have come.

For example, as I previously mentioned, I wanted to live away from Puerto Rico for at least a year. When I was working the family business, I could not do it. After we sold and I went to the Hoffman Process Retreat, the idea of living overseas and how much I had always wanted to do that popped up again and again. My wife and the kids and I tried to go away for a year. At the time, the girls were, I think, in fifth grade or about to go to sixth grade. I was starting to travel a lot and it wasn't the right time and we never did it.

THE HOFFMAN PROCESS

As per their website

The Hoffman Process is an eight-day intensive residential course of personal discovery and development. Please check their website www.hoffmaninstitute.org for more information.

That's why we decided to spend a whole summer in Boulder, Colorado, where we had a great time; it gave us the chance to be away from home together, perhaps for not as long as I had dreamed of being away, but it was a solution that worked for all of us, as a family, achieving our goal of being together in a way that did not uproot us and take my children away from their school. And we are a better, more experienced family because of it, because I never let go of this dream and instead continue to find a way to make it succeed for all of us.

Perhaps back then, right after selling the company, was the perfect time to go away for a year instead of thinking and wondering about what to do next in my life. I could have done it somewhere else and given my entire family the experience of living in another culture for a year or two. But again, we found a compromise, working together.

So it didn't happen exactly as I had once planned, but it's one of those things I offer as an example to everybody to help them ask themselves if they are doing what they want to do and to encourage them to write down their goals. They should talk to their spouses or partners and then think about the life they are living. What is it that they want to do with their life? People might surprise themselves once they open up about what they really want in life.

> ### *People might surprise themselves once they open up about what they really want in life.*

Sometimes we just think of family and responsibility. We just want to be good parents and give our children an education and move forward. We can talk all day about what else we want to instill in our children. We want to teach them integrity. We want to teach them great values, honesty, whatever it is that is important to us. If we don't think about it, we might miss what it is exactly that we want to teach them.

ROCKEFELLER'S CREDO AND THE YOUNG PRESIDENTS' ORGANIZATION

I belong to an organization called the Young Presidents' Organization, or YPO for short. Every year we have a forum retreat where we hire an outside facilitator or coach to guide us through the retreat.

Before going to one of our last retreats, our facilitator gave us a list of questions and an exercise to complete. We were given a lot of information along with questions to answer. The last question was about writing a personal credo. It had been a long day for me, and I could not believe the last question seemed the most difficult.

The question was based on the life of John D. Rockefeller Jr., one of the wealthiest men the world has ever known. Out facilitator told us that in 1961, a year after Rockefeller's death, a plaque inscribed with the famous "I believe" credo was installed at the Rockefeller Center in New York City where it still stands today. You'll find it at the end of the promenade leading from Fifth Avenue, just as you reach the sunken garden of the complex, the place with the ice-skating rink in the winter time, underneath the golden statue of Prometheus. It's in plain view but hard to see in reality. Thousands of tourists stand in front of this meaningful plaque every day, blocking it, actually, as they face away from it, posing in photos with Prometheus in the background. If most tourists took the time to read this plaque, I wonder how much more rewarding their trips to New York would be.

ROCKEFELLER'S CREDO

I believe in the supreme worth of the individual and in his right to life, liberty, and the pursuit of happiness. I believe that every right implies a responsibility; every opportunity, an obligation; every possession, a duty.

I believe the law was made for man and not man for the law; that government is the servant of the people and not their master. I believe in the dignity of labor, whether with head or hand; that the world owes no man a living, but that it owes every man an opportunity to make a living.

I believe that thrift is essential to well-ordered living and that economy is a prime requisite of a sound financial structure, whether in government, business, or personal affairs. I believe that truth and justice are fundamental to an enduring social order.

I believe in the sacredness of a promise, that a man's word should be as good as his bond; that character—not wealth or power or position—is of supreme worth.

continued...

I believe that the rendering of useful service is the common duty of mankind, and that only in the purifying fire of sacrifice is the dross of selfishness consumed and the greatness of the human soul set free.

I believe in an all-wise and all-loving God, named by whatever name, and that the individual's highest fulfillment, greatest happiness, and widest usefulness are to be found in living in harmony with his will.

I believe that love is the greatest thing in the world; that it alone can overcome hate; that it can and will triumph over might.

With this question, this final assignment to think about what we would leave for the world, the instructor asked us what we would want inscribed in stone as our personal credo. I started writing and I got really involved in the assignment. I feel it was one of the most rewarding assignments I have ever had, one that completely captured my imagination.

What I finished doing was what I call my own piece of art, what I really believe, my credo. Jofi's credo.

JOFI'S CREDO

I believe in love.

I believe in individuality; love your uniqueness.

I trust everyone until that person gives me a reason not to trust him again, and even with that, I will probably give him a second chance.

I help as much as I can.

Each one of us has the power, the will, to make of ourselves whatever we want to be; the only one stopping us is ourselves.

I believe in God.

I believe being a parent is the most precious gift God has given us, and with that comes family, an awesome bonus.

Sunrises and sunsets are there to be enjoyed.

Spend time with your loved ones as much as you can.

God made you just the way you are.

Follow your own heart, your own intuitions, not someone else's.

Find a passion in your life.

Be free as you can be.

Share your wealth with everyone. (I am not talking about money here, but your knowledge, happiness, abilities, etc.)

I bask in the smile of a young kid.

I believe in reading to your kid every single night. continued...

I believe in kissing your children, every single day, until your last day on this earth.

I believe in taking risks.

I know you can do it.

I want your friendship.

Give me a smile if I do not have one on my face when I see you.

Enjoy the present, this instant.

You have the power to change the world.

I am there for you.

I choose to believe I am here for a purpose; find that purpose.

I am much more than what your eyes can see.

I believe in forgiveness.

I believe in myself.

I believe in love.

This credo is something I strive to live by, and I always keep it in view.

This credo is something I strive to live by, and I always keep it in view. It's right here, next to my computer, on the wall, as I write this book. I see it every day. It's something that keeps reminding me of who I am, what my values are. I am always thinking of my credo and asking myself and checking on myself to see if I'm living the life I really want to live. Creating a personal credo has an impact on you. Even the act of writing down your credo has an impact beyond merely thinking about it. The effect is stronger. And that impact is strengthened each time you reread the credo to yourself. Your credo is something to live by.

It's something I have been very proud of creating ever since I did so last year. I talk about my personal credo everywhere and with every retreat facilitator or at every event I attend. I encourage everybody to write theirs. I'll give you an example. We wrote personal credos on a trip I took for teenagers in Arizona. We are talking about seventeen-, eighteen-, nineteen-year-old teenagers. It was really precious to hear their credos, from really technical or funny ones to others that were intensely serious and mature. They were what these teenagers believed in. Even at that seemingly young age, before all of life's experiences, young people can have credos about the life they want to live and how they want to live it, guiding them in their thoughts, plans, and decisions. Their true selves were coming out and it was a beauty to be there to experience it.

I think writing a credo really helps you to become your authentic self. It's kind of like bringing up to the surface who you really are. When you write it down, it's like "Wow!" Then you realize it and it hits you in the face. It kind of wakes you up to see if you are living the life that you say in your credo you believe in. It has a moving impact.

I simply believe that when you write your values down on paper, when you create your credo, and you see it there in black and white, it has a tremendous impact on you. You are the one who wrote that and it helps you internalize at a greater depth the message you are sending yourself. It's not about just thinking about it. The act of writing it down has a big effect on you.

We know that writing things down works. The thing is that it is often too late when we understand this process. Often people simply don't like to write, even if it will be of help to them in processing something.

So it goes simply beyond writing our credos down. The actual act of writing things down helps you to sort out your thoughts when they need to be sorted out or when you need to reassess things.

> ***The actual act of writing things down helps you to sort out your thoughts when they need to be sorted out.***

Now what I want is for you to grab a pen and paper, or perhaps switch on your computer or laptop. Even your iPad will do.

What's your personal credo? Take a few minutes to come up with values you believe in. Now take what you've written and paste it above your desk so that you always have this to refer to. Or paste it on the refrigerator—anywhere you know you're going to see it often.

Once you write down your credo and put it next to you on your office wall, your computer, or your refrigerator, it will help to remind you of what you believe in.

CHAPTER FIVE

Your Relationship with Yourself

We have talked a lot about how important it is to have a healthy relationship with your work life and with your family and the people you love.

Yet often the person you overlook in relationships is yourself. You often neglect your health and well-being, putting that of others above your own. It's important to maintain a balance even when you work hard. You cannot do anything unless you take care of yourself.

Many people I meet in the course of my coaching take their health for granted. They feel they have to work hard by doing more than enough, which they often think is never enough, for their family. If you think about it, there are always reasons to continue working harder. Through it all, we often don't take care of ourselves. The number-one person you should be taking care of is you.

The number-one person you should be taking care of is you.

We're taught at an early age not to be selfish, to always be thinking of other people, to share, to give our time, to do everything to please others.

What's missing in this discourse is that we never think about how we first have to take care of ourselves in order to take care of everyone else. If I become sick, I cannot work and put food on the table for my family. If I'm sick, I cannot take care of my spouse and my kids. If I'm out of shape, if I'm going to die young, I won't grow old and see my grandchildren. People are not aware of how taking care of themselves impacts how well they can take care of others.

A great, great example I always give about this is when there's an emergency in the airplane and the breathing masks come down. What do they tell you to do first? First, put the mask on yourself before you help another person. Simply put, if you don't do that first, you'll pass out and die, and you won't be able to help anybody.

I'll give you another example from scuba diving. They teach you that in an emergency you must first stop, breathe, think, and then act. If you just jump into the water, instead of having one casualty, we might have two casualties. We first have to take care of ourselves before we try to take care of somebody else.

We first have to take care of ourselves before we try to take care of somebody else.

People nowadays don't take time out for themselves, because they think that would be selfish. They don't want to take a moment once a week or once a month for their own physical and mental needs—for example, taking some time to read by themselves, taking time to catch a movie, whatever makes them feel replenished. People are simply not doing it because they feel they are taking time away from their family, from their spouse, from work, from whatever it is they feel is more important than themselves at any given moment.

YOUR HAPPY SELF

The thing is, when you do that, you are actually going to be able to give more of yourself, and more of what I like to call your happy self. You'll be a person who is more aware or more capable or willing to work when you have taken time to take care of yourself. We've seen that idea slowly develop in different companies with their meditation rooms or exercise rooms. Or they have time-outs for different kinds of breaks because people need to replenish themselves in order to take care of other responsbilities in life. Some companies even have nap rooms, realizing we all have different times when we need to rest, even if it is for fifteen or twenty minutes before we go back to our desks. Often, even when we feel overloaded, just those few short moments are enough to recharge our batteries.

I think adequate rest is important for your health, in addition to eating right as you do all you need to do.

I'll give you an example. I have done a few triathlons, training on Mondays, Wednesdays, and Fridays. At 5:00 a.m. I was already in the swimming pool. My life for the past two years has revolved around that. Then I realized I wasn't happy doing it. In fact, I realized I didn't even like it that much. I had simply gotten swept up with the Ironman fever just as so many others had in Puerto Rico.

Now I am in the process of organizing my athletic life to see what it is I really want to do. What kind of exercise I want to do, when I want to do it, how much I'm going to be able to do. By reexamining and organizing my exercise time, I find I am now really enjoying my mornings. I wake up, I meditate, I check on my pet fish, I check my patio. Now, I wake up more relaxed, and I take this "me" time every morning.

During the time it took me to write this book, I found out about CrossFit. It is functional training with high intensity. Every workout is different and you are always challenging yourself. I love it. There are great people in my group, and there is great camaraderie; we all support each other.

At the same time, I'm taking care of myself. People who know I don't have the intense regimen I once had tell me, "Oh, but you haven't gained any weight." Well, I'm taking care of myself. That I'm not exercising the way I used to doesn't mean I'm going to get fat and out of shape. I take care of myself, and I am even more aware of doing so because I am not exercising. I think it's very important to be conscious of this.

I love working on my patio in the open air. I also want to learn how to do bonsai—the art of cultivating small Japanese trees—because I think it's very reflective, very calming. I learned from a friend over dinner one night how relaxing it is for him. This friend has been doing bonsai ever since he finished medical school. Over the last twenty years, he has grown more than thirty-five bonsai trees and he simply loves it. At dinner, it was a revelation. I realized "Whoa! I want to do that. I'm going to see if I can take some classes and start with my first one and see how it goes."

I need to start figuring out what other things I want to do for myself. I found that I really enjoy working in my house, on my patio, with all my things there. In the past, I never used to do that. That's one outlet for relaxation and being by myself. And there are many more activities that I can find, that all of us can find, depending on our own unique circumstances.

I also now have a space in my home that I strictly use as my office. It hasn't been decorated. I don't have anything personal in it. To get started, I just found a chair and a table that we already had in the house and I placed them in a spare room. I enjoy working there at home when I am not traveling or in the company office, so that I can balance work with being home with the family, and taking my breaks with them. My goal is to maximize my time there, and thus with them. As I travel often, it is important for me to make sure I am with the family as much as I can be.

The happier I am, the more productive I feel.

As an example, the other day, I had a phone call at 7:00 a.m., which I took in my home office instead of having to go to the company office early. That is the sort of change I am making in my life in order to take care of myself. The happier I am, the more productive I feel. Everybody else in my life is going to benefit, from my clients to my spouse to my kids—everybody. It's really rewarding to be able to do things this way.

We need to think about this more often: how time for ourselves, whether a coffee break, or a real vacation, benefits others because it benefits ourselves.

Time for ourselves, whether a coffee break, or a real vacation, benefits others because it benefits ourselves.

An old-fashioned word for this—especially when it comes to something like my friend's bonsai plants and the little things that we love to do—is *hobby*. I think it's important to find a hobby, one or two things that you really love to do away from your family and your work. Time simply flies when you are enjoying such activities. In my case, I have found enjoyment through working on my patio and exercising.

I'll give you an example from my own father. I used to joke about his needing a hobby because it seemed he would have nothing to do in retirement. Now that he is retired, I feel he's sometimes bored. He plays golf, which he always did, but it's not as if you can do this the whole day every day. He's reading more and spending time with his grandkids, and that's what I'm talking about. Developing a hobby you can do for the rest of life is powerful.

Developing a hobby you can do for the rest of life is powerful.

For example, I want to learn how to play the piano, or the guitar, or maybe even the drums. That's something that's on my list. I wish I could do it today. I wish I could do a lot of things today, but at the end of the day, I know it's simply impossible. I don't have the time. I have it as a thought, as a desire. I am conscious of it, keeping it in the front row of my thoughts, so that when the time comes, I'm going to make it happen. I look at it as something very different from sports, my usual way of passing the time. I have never learned any instrument, and that is a huge part of the appeal.

Taking up a hobby, finding something new to do, challenging ourselves, is also a way to stay sharp, to keep our mind at work, even as the hobby relaxes us. Of course, you want to make sure that when you take up a new hobby, it doesn't result in a challenging situation, or you'll go overboard. I always point out that when people do Ironman, even traveling for it, a lot of your time is taken in training—a lot. We are talking about three sports and, basically, you have to train every single day. If you have a family, it takes time from them. It's important to challenge yourself, but what are you missing in your life because of that? What is it that you're not taking care of because you're training? I'm not trying to judge anybody here. I'm just trying to bring up a topic to reflect on. A hobby should be something that you enjoy, that relaxes you, not another arena in addition to work where you always feel you must compete. That simply defeats the purpose of it.

There are many things we might want to do, many things we want to strive to be better at. For example, right now, I am working on a new running routine and trying to incorporate it into my schedule. It's something that I feel will be right for me, once I start doing it. Still, I don't want to put pressure on myself to do it. I wanted to start a couple of weeks ago, yet I didn't, and that's okay. I wanted to run yesterday and it was too late and I couldn't. It's okay. Any day now I'm going to start. I'm going to start cleaning up my schedule, but I am not punishing myself with bad thoughts for not yet having done so.

I believe the important thing is to learn from something and continue moving forward. I'm not saying this to give you an excuse to delay exercising, but we must give ourselves permission to be human. We don't have to be so hard on ourselves. When we miss a day, as sometimes happens, we tend to criticize ourselves because we naturally want to do our best and do what we have to do as long as it's not unethical or illegal. Criticism is negative thinking. There are enough people in our lives who will be critical of us. We want to make sure that we are the last to do that to ourselves. There is a point

I want to make very clear, so clear that I think it's important to restate it now that we are at the end of the chapter. Simply put, the better you are to yourself, the better you are to other people, the better you are to the people you're working with.

We must give ourselves permission to be human.

---

*The better you are to yourself,
the better you are to other people.*

You can be better to yourself in many ways: looking after your health, enjoying hobbies, exercise, and so forth. Remember that taking time for yourself makes you a better you for other people.

I believe once you take care of yourself first, once you are at your best—meaning that you are healthy, you're open minded, you're doing everything you can to take care of yourself—you are going to be in a better position to help everybody else around you do what they love to do. Your influence, your output for those around you, is going to be more positive. All of those you love and work with are going to benefit from a better you.

CHAPTER SIX

Your Relationship with Money

We have talked about our relationships with other people and with ourselves. Now we will ask the question some people think is even more personal: What is your relationship with money?

When you think about money, what do you think about? This obsession with money and how much you are making can overtake you. It can even make you unhappy with doing something you thought would be fulfilling.

How Much Is Enough?

When they talk about money, some people have no idea how much is enough. I want to start by saying I don't think there's anything wrong with making money and having lots of money. But we should be aware of the effect money has on us, on the way we live our lives, and on the way we treat other people. If you are working, working, and working, and your excuse for never being with your family is that you are working for them, making more and more money, are you really doing that for them? Or is it that you want to do it and don't want to be with your family? Or are you even aware of what you are doing? These things are important to know.

Again, everything I'm saying in this book is to help people become aware, open up, and wake up to the life they are living. We need to check all the different arenas of our lives. Say to yourself, "Yeah, this one's checked. This is what I want to do. This is the way I know it's going to happen."

We must know whether we are working for the benefits money can bring us, or solely for the money itself. Are we relegating our family to the back burner while we work? Are we neglecting them because we really want to make more money and more money?

Then again, what is it you want to do with all your money? You can have all the money in the world and do great things, give to great charities, get involved. I'm very happy to see a lot of people who have a lot of money give a lot back. I think that's very commendable, and I am proud of all those people who do that. Some wealthy people don't do that, and I wonder what they are going to do with their money. Maybe they are going to take it home, maybe take it with them when they die. I don't know. It's kind of weird. You know you can't take it with you, unless you line your casket with it. And what good would that do?

People handle their money in all kinds of different ways. Some people have a lot of money that they don't spend on anything. Some people have very little money, yet they have a good time with it and give to good causes, which, I think, shows a great sense of balance. If you have it, you can enjoy it—fantastic! If you can also share it with the less fortunate, even better.

Studies show that unless you are really poor, meaning that $1,000 is going to make a big difference to you, or you are starving and need money to stay alive, money does not make you happy.

MONEY DOESN'T BRING YOU HAPPINESS

People tell me, "How could you sell the family business? I would never sell it." Yet I know they would sell their family business if they really wanted to, if the circumstances were right. It's a question of putting the money from the sale of the business to good use and doing something with your life. And that, for me, became the most important thing. It was an important revelation that I could do something different in life after we had sold the company.

I'm always wondering why people who can sell and want to sell don't. Oftentimes people might be afraid or don't know what to do next.

You see this situation a lot with families and businesses in which the biggest issue is money. Money brings the fight into the family. It creates break-ups among brothers, sisters, parents, uncles. It is very, very sad. You get to the point where money doesn't bring happiness, and then you're fighting because of money. Wow! Why do we have to be so selfish about it? Why can't we just talk about it and work it out?

If the families who fight about money had none, they would probably be happier, spending the weekend together, enjoying each other. Because of money, they don't talk to each other, or they are always fighting, or whatever. What did that money bring to that family? Tell me. Did it bring them happiness? Or did it bring them just a family that is not together, a broken family? That's very important to think about, and you should make sure that money doesn't affect your friendships and especially your family.

More Money Equals More Issues

We are going through a remodeling in my house. We moved from a small house to a big house on a large lot. The more things we do to the house, the more issues arise. I have the money to spend on various improvements, but I end up creating more problems for myself. So, I have decided to turn my attitude around. I told myself I was lucky to have enough money to spend on nice things for my house.

Yes, some things are going to happen. Things are not going to be perfect. Contractors are going to miss appointments to go over construction work. Others may not do carpentry work correctly the first time. Yet, in the end, everything will be okay.

I changed my attitude from "poor me, all these things are happening to me" to "I am lucky to be in this situation; let me just work on it and appreciate what I have. It's not the end of the world that the doors were not done the way I wanted them, or there's a space that needs to get fixed, or the bricks and mortar aren't done properly, with the edges fitting smoothly. It can be fixed. We can work around it. It's not the end of the world. There are more important things in life, and really, I should feel lucky to have the financial ability to spend on a house renovation project."

Now, after hitting my head against the wall a lot of times, I am more patient. I feel more grateful about what I have and the situation that I am in. I'm more relaxed, more forgiving, and I take it easy with everything that is happening at the house. It's like people divorcing while constructing or remodeling a big house. It can get bad. You have to be really, really careful. Thank God I woke up to it. I'm aware of it now, so I am more relaxed about it.

For example, my wife and I fought over the furniture we were going to buy, and then we decided we would take a break. The house is going to stay the way it is right now, and we're going to take a two- or three-month break. When we're ready, we'll go back to it.

Why should we continue fighting and damaging our good relationship because of furniture? We should be enjoying this time together, deciding which furniture to buy, which sofa, which TV. It's not a life or death situation, nothing to be worked-up over.

Money can be poison to people and family relationships. When you spend money, do you define yourself by money, by how much you make? Are you jealous of people with more money? Do you treat people differently because of money? Is flying first class versus coach about prestige for you?

I believe money can be the source of great things in life. Yet, at the same time, it can be poison for you, the family, relationships, if you really are not aware of how you are reacting to it. Because they have money, some people act as if they should have preferential treatment, or they expect a lot from other people. Why is that? What makes them better? Are your values, the way you behave, influenced by the amount of money you have?

When I had a BMW, I was a snob. I felt more important because I was driving a BMW. I didn't like that feeling, to be honest, so I don't have a BMW anymore. I never had it for that long anyway, but my snobbish attitude was something I became aware of in the course of owning a BMW. Some would say, "Why? Why, just because I can own a BMW, do I feel like this?" It's something that I became aware of and I fixed it, so I no longer have a BMW. That's a small example of how money has affected me.

I know from my travels there is an obvious difference in the way a flight attendant treats first-class passengers versus coach passengers. Is it fair? Is it not fair? First-class passengers pay more; passengers in coach class pay less. They give you more in first class; in coach they give you less. Shouldn't the treatment be the same? Shouldn't you treat a human being just the same no matter who he or she is?

Shouldn't you treat a human being just the same no matter who he or she is?

Why do people feel they have to treat wealthy people differently? What is it about wealthy people? I have been learning to treat everybody equally, regardless of social class. I feel truer to myself when I do that.

We should be aware of these issues with money: how it defines us, how it can be used the wrong way, poisoning us in our relationships with our families, our friends, and ourselves.

CHAPTER SEVEN

Your Relationship with Work

This will be one of the longer chapters in this book. Some of the material I know I have touched on in different ways. Work, however, is where we have some of our greatest fears, along with our greatest need to feel validated.

I am going to tell you a little story about a time after we sold the family business, a time when I was not working in the general sense of the word.

After I graduated from college, I began the process of deciding what to do. Instead of going back out to work in an office job or in the family insurance business, I started working as a teaching tennis pro. Right after graduation, I went to work in Vermont for the rest of the summer, and then I went back home and taught tennis there. Then, I spent a year teaching tennis in Hilton Head, South Carolina. My family asked me when I was coming home. They asked me to return to Puerto Rico to work there instead. It made sense for them to ask that. But it also made sense for me to look for something else for a year. Why go through all the hassle of working for somebody else, of interviewing, trying to find a job? It wasn't for want of knowing what else to do and it wasn't because I'd given up on myself. Nor was it about letting others influence what I wanted to do at that time. It was about following my own path.

I returned home eventually, working in the family business, and I had a great time. I learned a lot. I spent a lot of time with my dad. In fact, my dad taught me everything that he knew. It was a very enriching and rewarding experience: building a business and having a positive effect on all our employees and our employees' families, on our clients, on the relationships that we built because of our business. I even loved all the traveling we did because of the family business.

Sometimes, at the family business, I felt I was simply hanging out, simply putting in time. I realized that wasn't me. Perhaps I felt that way because I didn't know what else to do. I understand now that I didn't appreciate things as I should have. It wasn't that I didn't give 100 percent. I did, but I had no passion for it. I didn't give my best because my passion wasn't in my work there. I wasn't as into it as my dad was. I only realized all that after we sold the company and I knew there were choices I had to make, on my own.

I had many thoughts as I contemplated my next career. Finding out what I wanted to do made me realize many things. I said, "Wow! Now I understand a lot of things that happened while I was in the family business." I understood because of what I had decided to do about coaching and all the other things I wanted to do: speaking, writing, helping people. There are parts of my current career that I don't want to do, such as administrative or organizational work—for example, the notes you have to compile before you write a book, even the one you see in your hand; or the notes you have to make before you write a speech; or things you have to do before you go coaching. I just love the actual coaching, but I realize the administrative work is necessary. It is the necessary preparation I must do to reap the benefits of what I love to do, the process of becoming, before the actual doing.

The process of becoming, before the actual doing.

Remember what I said about opening a restaurant and the frustrations you can encounter? If you are passionate about it, it doesn't matter what's going to happen. When I look back, I see all the time my new career has taken. Altogether, the preparation for coaching began three years ago. I believe the timing was right. I appreciate the fact that the time I spent in preparation helps me fine-tune this new path I have taken.

Many different things have helped me come to this point. It's very hard to pinpoint the exact moment, the exact catalyst. My new path has fallen into place slowly. Everything that has happened in my life in the last few years has contributed in some way, big or small, to my feeling more prepared for what I want to do.

I feel it inside me, the passion that I have to do this. Again, I do not know what the ending will be. I know I'm going to enjoy it and give 100 percent of myself to it. My passion is there and it is going to work out.

I just have to trust my intuition about this. I'm doing well. I hear it from people all the time. I just have to move forward, being aware of what I'm doing and not letting anything else stop me on my path.

I had a particularly hard time because I was in a family business. Many more obligations were placed on me. I had more responsibility, perhaps, and some might say I carried familial guilt. There was baggage that might not have existed if I had been employed by a company that had nothing to do with the family business, where things would have been less personal, and where I would not have lived at home with the same people I worked with.

At the same time, we all share many of the same circumstances that keep us at work, no matter where we are employed. We have debts, obligations, expectations, all of which might make us think we need to stay where we are.

Some people might think, "This is my job. This is what I can do. There's no way out, so I just move forward, unhappy." I believe there are two ways about it. You can change your outlook and realize the impact that change of outlook has on whatever it is you do, or you can give serious thought to making a career change. With everything that goes through your head, have you really sat down to think about, even consider, a change?

You have to ask yourself what else you can do. How can you get out of the rut you're in? Many people are unhappy in their work. If they do not change their job, what can they do to live a happier, more meaningful life? It all depends on them. If they want to make the best of it, they must focus on what is good about their position. If they are just going to be negative in everything that they do, their situation is going to be negative no matter where they work. If they appreciate what they have, all the good in it, things are going to be much better.

When you appreciate the good, the good appreciates.

There is a saying that when you appreciate the good, the good appreciates. Think about that phrase and let it linger for a moment. That's the thing. We go through life not appreciating all the things we have right in front of us, because they are there every single day. But when we don't have them—boom! That's when we start missing them.

Debts, Obligations, and Expectations

There are many reasons why people stay where they are at work, everything from personal debt to expectations that other people have for them. Why do people stay or what makes them think that they made the wrong decision when they leave?

Well, here are some of the points people sometimes make to me when I ask this question. They miss being the boss; they have no one to lead. This is particularly the case when people are owners or former owners of a company. I have heard from others that this kind of person is just another millionaire without a company. Some people hold on to their business simply because it has become their identity, as if they are nobody without it.

Things change drastically when you sell your own business. I think a lot of people are afraid of change. Some say, "Why change when everything is going so well?"

They can't give up being the boss. Having people to lead, to supervise, to tell what to do—they want to continue having all that. Sadly, I think a lot of people identify themselves with the company. If they sell their company, they feel they might lose their identity.

Once they leave the company, they seem to turn into different people. They don't seem to realize they are much more than the company. I think it's really great that they had that company—they built it, or they bought it, or whatever—but they're not the company. Their identity is not the company. They are completely amazing human beings with great qualities who created the companies they have now sold. You might say a little piece of them goes with the company and that's great, but it's not them.

They are completely amazing human beings with great qualities who created the companies they have now sold.

It is not the sum total of who they are. I believe a lot of people have that difficulty of separating who they are from the company they own. They might feel they are nobody if they sell it.

I tell people things change when they sell their company. Of course they change. People don't call them any more for lunch. There are no more business trips. The phone doesn't ring as before. After selling my own company, I have always joked that the only person I really, really miss is my computer guy, the guy I could call any time, who would come to my house to fix the computers at home. That's it, for me. But that's just me. I laugh about it, thinking back.

Some people have a harder time. In my case, I chose a completely different career path from what I had before. Maybe it's easier for me now that I'm away from the business culture I was immersed in. Then again, I am still myself, and I am working to be more authentic, to be more myself, to find the true me. That's what I do in my personal life and my professional career. I help people do that in my new role as a coach.

It goes beyond missing being the boss. It's about other aspects of work too, seemingly intangible things that are side products of company business. They include business lunches, holiday parties, gifts, whether from coworkers or other companies trying to woo your business.

But things change when you're no longer at the company, when you're no longer the boss. The holiday parties and lunches are gone;

people don't call you anymore for advice or simply to check in and be in touch. It seems the respect you once garnered as an executive is no longer there. The gifts you received at Christmas from other companies and clients, and the joy you had in picking gifts out for others have gone. It's a very different scenario now. But when we change fields, when we change paths, we have an opportunity to do a lot of good in this world. We should all find a way to take advantage of that.

LIFE CHANGES

Are there things holding you back from making a life change? What would you do if you had all the time and money in the world?

> ### *What would you do if you had all the time and money in the world?*

It goes back to the same thing of reflecting on the life that you're living and the way you live your life. People really get stuck to their company, and they don't want to let go for whatever reason. There's always a good excuse. For example, owners believe they won't get the money they think their company's worth. I think that if they are at the point where they can sell their company and live a very fulfilling life afterward, selling is worth reflecting on.

Faced with these questions, what would you love to do if there were no obstacles? What would you do if you had all the money and time in the world? By answering these questions, you will get a lot of great insight into yourself. Did you answer these questions without blocking any answers or thinking about it too much? Did you write your answers down right away? What shows up is what's deep inside you. It might be right. It might be wrong. It might be crazy, but it is what is there inside you. Writing your answer down will help you to reflect on your answer.

For me, what comes to mind immediately is the movie starring Morgan Freeman and Jack Nicholson, *The Bucket List*.

Jack Nicholson is all about making money and Morgan Freeman has this bucket list. They ended up in the same hospital room. They are both about to die. They have six months or a year to live. Morgan Freeman has the bucket list and Jack Nicholson has the money to make the items on that list happen. Doing all these things brings him alive.

That's kind of like a wake-up call. Why wait for something drastic to happen in your life before you really think about the life that you're living? Go ahead and do the things you want to do. Why wait to do them? Why don't you do them now while you control your own destiny?

> ***Why wait for something drastic to happen in your life before you really think about the life you are living?***

In the case of the movie, the two men have to act immediately because they have little time left to live. They go ahead. There is no tomorrow for them. Why do we always save the good one for a great occasion? Why keep the nice shirt for a special situation? Use it now. Enjoy it. There might be no tomorrow. It's not about being pessimistic. Enjoy the present. Enjoy the now. Make the most of it and move on in life.

Move through life.

Rethinking the Meaning of Money

It takes a while to realize that more money might not bring more happiness. What makes you happier than $100,000, $500,000, one million dollars? What gets in the way when we think about finances and jobs? The issue is money, and this belief, this obsession, that more money will make you happier.

I think we live in a society in which too many people think money is going to make them happy. Then when we have all this money, or whatever material thing it is, how much is really enough? It's not going to solve problems. Money can solve issues, but in the end it's never enough. When you get right down to it, having more money does not make you feel better. Research shows us that money doesn't give you happiness. It doesn't mean because you have more money than I do that you're happier than I am.

How much is really enough?

I think that from childhood we have this idea that we need to make money to be happy and have everything that we want in life. That is sad, I think.

For example, the basketball player Ray Allen signed with the Miami Heat for around $3 million less a year, because he wasn't looking for money. Yes, he was looking to be part of a championship team, so he signed with the world champions, leaving around $10 million on the table. Imagine that. And most people forget about Lebron James. He left a lot of money on the table to join a championship contending team.

We might say that they already had money, so it was no big deal for them. We might believe that, compared to us, it didn't really matter, because Ray Allen might not consider $10 million to be as much as you or I would consider it to be. Maybe we will never look at $10 million deals. Maybe for you and me, $10,000 might not be so much; forget about that $10,000. It's all relative, and Allen didn't think about the money. Rather, he just thought about where he would be happier, which, I think, at the end of the day, is where we all want to be. We want to be happy in whatever we do and wherever we are. At the same time, we have to be careful how money changes us. Money is not a bad thing, as long as we put it to a good use.

It's not bad to have money, and to make lots of money. I just believe that what you do with it will tell me who you are. What kind of person are you when it comes to money?

What kind of person are you when it comes to money?

Some people are just making money because they want to, and basically that's it for them. There are some people who don't even want to spend it on themselves. Then what are they working so hard for? My take on it is that if you make money and you give back to the community, to your employees, to your family, you can have fun with it. It is in this way that you can see how happy it can make you and others around you.

You can do noble things with your money, but if you start using that money to feel entitled, thinking that you are better than other people, you aren't going the right way about it.

Some families split up over money. It's also interesting that some people feel guilty over money, over having money and talking about it, and I can understand that from my own experience. A few years ago I was going to meet a friend of mine, the father of one of my daughter's friends. In order to recognize him, I asked him to describe the car he'd be driving. He said, "I drive a Toyota." But when he arrived, he was in a Mercedes Benz.

I just feel he was too humble or felt bad telling me he had a Mercedes. For my part, I don't think he felt comfortable driving that car. The biggest clue, of course, was that he couldn't say, "I drive a Mercedes Benz."

It's the opposite of someone who brags about what he owns. Here instead—and there is something wrong with this as well—sometimes we are made to feel guilty for having money, guilty for being successful, as if it does not suit us. Some people don't fly at all; some people fly in coach class; some people fly in business class; and some people have their own planes. There's nothing wrong with that. If you have a plane, I'm very happy for you. I have friends with planes, and I love flying with them. I'm very happy that they can have and enjoy what they have earned. They should not be ashamed of that.

At the same time, money can cause a lot of problems for people. And the question is what for? What is it about money that does this to people? I hear it in inheritance fights among siblings or when people are getting divorced. What is the issue? Money this, the money that. In the end, I don't know why money creates so many issues for people.

Even the Bible talks about this issue. But the phrase is not "money is the root of all evil," as many people misquote it, but "love of money is the root of all evil." In other words, it's not the object, but what we do with the object, our relationship with the object, that is the issue.

"Love of money is the root of all evil."

I once had an issue with driving a BMW, much like my friend with the Mercedes. I was happy that I made money, but the outward sign of my money, the car I was driving, felt ostentatious, as if it were more than I needed to show to others. I didn't want to feel like that. I just wanted to be myself.

For me, money is about home, family, and community. I want to be true to my home, to my family, and to my surrounding community. That's what I want to do with my success in whatever I do in life. For me, the importance is in giving back. I'm happy just helping people. That's why I decided to become a coach. Recently, a fellow YPO member called me about a referral for another coach who is a very good friend of mine.

After I explained to him that my friend would be a great choice for his company, I felt so good. This is something I feel I could do every day. I could have as many twenty people call me to talk about other people and how good they are. Recommending others, letting people know how good they are, that brings me alive. Helping others creates a sense of my own well-being, for my health, for my own emotions, for my happiness.

SELF-CHECK

There's a phrase I sometimes use, the *self-check*. It is a self-assessment. These are different questions you can ask yourself to do a self-check to determine how things are for you at a given moment. How's my relationship with money? How do I feel about it? How does it affect me? Am I obsessed with money? How much is enough? Have I really sat down and thought about it? If you're married, have you talked about money with your spouse? What is right for you? What is right for both of you?

For some people, just having enough money to get by is fine. Maybe, for other people, having $1 million of cash in the bank is fine. For other people, $100 million is the right amount. It varies. In the end, it is all about what you do with it, how you give back to the community, and how you give back to yourself and your family. I think that's what really counts when it comes to money.

And there is a self-check we can do when it comes to money and the relationship with your family. It's a startling question, one that almost brings us to the Midas legend of ancient Greece about the king who was very greedy until he lost his daughter when he turned her by accident into a statue of gold. At that point, he wanted to return all his riches just to have her back.

Today I would ask, in place of this legend, is there any amount of money I could give you to make you forget about your family? I am sure your answer is that no amount of money could make you do that.

Yet, in many ways, people forget about their families in pursuit of money, often giving the excuse that they work hard only for the sake of their families—a strange Catch-22 situation.

It's this aspect of the confusion many of us experience in our pursuit of money that is at the heart of this chapter. Rethink your relationship with money, and all your other relationships will improve. Above all, the relationship with your precious family will benefit the most from this assessment.

CHAPTER NINE

Your Relationship with Family

For me, family is the most important thing. If you're married, it's your spouse and your kids who matter. If you're not, then perhaps it's your immediate family—sister, brother, parents—who matter. There are many kinds of familial relationships and all have meaning for those in them. I think, for many people, the time when they feel most alive is usually when they are with their families.

> ***The time when they feel most alive is usually when they are with their families.***

At the same time, we should not take our family for granted. So many people are on cruise control in their relationship with their family or close friends. We should be aware of that, and we should be aware of how much time we spend with our family. Sometimes we think we can go away and expect family and friends to be there, waiting for us to return, as if they were stuck in time without us. I think I mentioned I travel a lot. I make sure when I am home I have time for everything that I need to do.

When we think about the relationship between family and work, we realize a lot of people spend a lot of time at work. Actually, I think we spend more time at work than with our family. If you take it to the next level, if your workday is longer than the typical eight hours, you have even less time for your family. It means you must be more conscientious about the value of the time you spend with them and be able to find more ways to increase that time, whenever and wherever possible.

When people are on their death bed and are asked what they regret, and what they would do all over again, what is their number-one response? Studies have found that the answer always is—and it comes too late—"I wish I had spent more time with my family." No one has said, "I wish I had spent more time at the office."

Yet, that's what a lot of people do. In general, a lot of people do that because they have this mentality that they must always be working and working and doing better and better in a never-ending cycle, a rat race. You are stuck on the wheel, but the faster you go, the more you stay in the same place. Fortunately, I think the new generation is beginning to look at work in a different way.

Partly it is because of the economy. Young people have more time with friends and family because of the way things are. In addition, it is also about technology: many people are able to work from home in ways unavailable even a generation ago. Advances have also been made in the area of paternity and maternity leave, because parents are more concerned with raising their children.

Young people today are concerned with more than just a job or a career in a company with potential for growth. For many, it's about living a healthy, balanced life based on their values and what it is that they want to do, what kind of life they want to have.

Workers in the upcoming generation are not thinking about being restrained by whatever career they choose.

Workers in the upcoming generation are not thinking about being restrained by whatever career they choose. Instead, for many, it's more a case of wanting to decide for themselves what they want to do, how they're going to do it, when they'll do it, and then living the kind of life they want to live. At least that's what they are trying to do, which is something I wholeheartedly agree with. I think all of us can learn from this younger generation.

In the past, it was just work, work, work, and coming home for the family. That was it, and then women did the same. I believe, now, there's more to it. You have got to take care of yourself. You have got to take care of your family, your work, everything. So I think it's more balanced than before.

DATE NIGHT

That brings me to telling you a little more about date night with my wife. It's something we do that makes us feel young and connected. It's the time when we throw away everything else that we're doing and just concentrate on each other, and it's as if we're kids dating again. I love to share this story with everybody, and it is a point I make as both a coach and as a husband.

My wife and I go out on Wednesday nights, although we have thought of moving our dates to Thursday, an easier day for both of us because our children have fewer commitments on Thursdays.

One of the things we like to do is go to the movies and then dinner together. It's just us spending our time together, catching up on the week, catching up about the kids, about each other and our work lives, all the questions we once asked each other when we were young. It is as if we get to know each other all over again. It's just a time for the two of us to be together.

It is not that we wouldn't want to be with our kids. It's not that we don't want to recognize the entire family, but it is time when we want to be with each other, knowing that we need time for ourselves.

I'll share with you this anecdote about date night as experienced by a friend of mine. He told me, "Yes, yes, I don't know what's wrong, but I do that with my wife. Once a week we go to this place and we hang out. We have a great time."

"This place" means where everybody's eating, drinking, and having a good time. It's kind of like going to the main square in your city, or to the shopping mall, and seeing a lot of friends and winding up talking to everybody. What it looks like to me is that they get there together and they start talking to everybody. At the end of the night they see each other again and go back home.

They seemed to have no time together, no time for just the two of them with no distractions. I explained to my friend, "No, no, no. The idea is for you two to go out alone, with no one else you know around. It's not about seeing friends or sharing with other people. This time is just for you, for each other." Every couple needs this, this time to be alone together.

For example, I have already mentioned how we did it from the family perspective, spending six weeks in Boulder, Colorado, a few summers ago—only the five of us, as a family unit, no one else, just my wife, and I, and our three children. No family visited. No friends visited. We had a great time and formed great memories together. It's something we're going to cherish forever. It was just about our family. We have our family trip with my parents and my sisters. We have our time with my wife's family in Panama, but this time was just about us five, about the great memories that we will cherish forever, without commitments forced on us by other people. You can have that with the family, and you can have that with your spouse.

One thing you always want to remember about your family, and about your spouse, is to never take them for granted.

One thing you always want to remember about your family, and about your spouse, is to never take them for granted. And they will always be there for you. Over a lifetime, we may have many careers, but hopefully, we will always have our one family and our spouse.

It's important to always be there for them. In the course of being married to my wife, I've already had two different careers, and now I am launching a new one. The family will always be there, but the people who work with me might not always be there as I make this transition in life. Of course, we do know people get divorced, but if we are always there for the family, in whatever capacity that may be, we will always have them there for us.

If you're married, your spouse and your kids will be there, no matter what you do. No matter what work throws at you, no matter if you get fired, if you quit your job, or you change careers, they will be the one constant in your life. Let's give our relationship with our family the importance it requires. Sometimes we forget and take for granted what we love the most. We should always be aware of that.

I think also people misconstrue this concept of quality time: time alone with the spouse, time alone with the children, even ten minutes with them, helping them with their homework, or reading to them at night.

This is also an important way to better understand your children, and to understand their friends, the other children they are hanging out with.

In terms of being with family and talking a lot with our children, we have to also be aware of really being there with them. If we cannot turn off the phone and the e-mail to be with them, we're lying to ourselves that we are there with them. They can feel that and they know it. At the end of the day, kids just want time with their parents. I have already mentioned the friend of mine who says he spends time with his child, but in reality, he's on his Blackberry, ignoring his son who is right next to him.

One thing to remember about children is that for them, family time is more important than material things. They're not really thinking about the big house even though it's nice. They're not thinking about the pool even though, yes, that's nice too. It's about the time that they want. Recently, I told my son to brush his teeth— no, no, no, he won't. So I tell him, "Brush your teeth and I'll take you to school in the morning, just you, so we can have time talking in the car." My wife usually takes the kids, and so he was worried I would break my promise. So, he told me to pinky promise.

My son was probably the first kid in school that day because he was there so early. Your kids just want to be with you, and you to be with them. I think I have already mentioned that you see some parents taking their kids to school and that's great. But if you're talking on the phone while holding their hand, and you go on cruise control, the kids know. They feel it. They realize that although you're there with them, you're really not.

Just be aware of that. Why can't that phone call wait—you know, unless you're a doctor? Let's be there with them when we're there with them.

Let's be there with them when we're there with them.

KNOWING YOUR CHILDREN'S FRIENDS

I also want to stress that time with your children also allows you to know better who their friends are, who they are hanging out with. My wife and I were talking about this the other day, about how it was when we were young. Friends called our houses when we were kids, and my mother or my father would shout, "Hey, Jofi, Carlos is calling you." Nowadays, with cell phones, Facebook, texting, and everything else kids are using, we don't know who they're talking to. Kids can connect to their friends and entirely skip the parent filter.

Kids can connect to their friends and entirely skip the parent filter.

It's important to talk to your kids all the time, know who they're talking to and know who their friends are. In my house, we believe that, rather than letting the children go to their friends' houses, which of course they often do, we prefer to have them home. We get to meet all their friends, talk to them, and spend time with them.

It's another way of spending time with your child's group, allowing your kids to feel comfortable being themselves, and having fun. I think it's great to be part of that. I'll give you an anecdote.

The other day a friend had a party at his house for his daughter's birthday, which my own daughters attended. My wife asked me to pick up the girls when the party was over. I was told they would be waiting for me in front of the house. However, when I arrived, I did not see them, so I went into the house, where the teenagers were still partying.

Now, my teenage daughters were embarrassed that their father had come inside the house during the party. One of my daughters sent over a friend of hers to tell me how she felt. They were having fun, and she and I fought about it afterward. But I left the party, letting her stay longer. I was young once. I understood. Sometimes it can be terrifying to have your parents show up at a party! However, everybody said "Hi!" to me. I have been told I am a cool dad by many of my daughters' friends. To me, even if they were embarrassed, the other kids did not seem to mind.

Of course, my daughters, being teenagers, were mortified that I had walked into the party. So when we finally saw each other, my daughters laughed about it—but yelled at me at the same time. "No, no, no. You don't do that." The important thing, embarrassment aside, is that my daughters and I are able to talk about it like that. For my part, if I feel I made a mistake, I do my best to apologize to my kids. Communicate—always communicate with your kids. I think it's key to a great relationship between parent and child, especially in the teenage years when it is very important for children to express how they feel.

You always must make sure you are approachable to your children.

You always must make sure you are approachable to your children. That is how you become a resource. That is how you know you are protecting your children. When you have this quality time with your family and when your family really needs you, they won't be afraid to come to you. They will be able to approach you on any issue, no matter how serious or embarrassing it is.

I want to share other stories about family togetherness and learning about my children's friends. One is about my nine-year-old son. I go to his classroom, and I start talking to his friends, girls and boys. I go around the classroom and ask, "So tell me, how is José doing? Is he behaving? Is he talking too much?" And all the children fill me in on how he is doing in school.

One relationship we are trying to integrate in our family life concerns my parents. Even though we see them often, my wife and I would like to schedule a day a week when they go to pick up the kids at their extracurricular activities, and then we all have dinner together. We started doing this, but my father's schedule did not allow it, so now we are scrambling to see how we can make it happen.

From a logistical point of view, it makes a lot of sense. Think back to when you were a kid, and think of your life now if you have kids. Think of the happiness kids feel when they interact with their grandparents. The happiness this relationship with grandparents promotes and the way these generations connect are very important components of kids' development.

We often rush around, not thinking of how quickly our kids will grow up before our very eyes. We put off today what we think we can do tomorrow and then we put it off again.

We put off today what we think we can do tomorrow and then we put it off again.

This is all in a very old song, "The Cat's in the Cradle," by Harry Chapin. My favorite lines from that song are: "And as I hung up the phone it occurred to me, He'd grown up just like me. My boy was just like me."

The song is from the early 1970s, but its theme is eternal. It has a lot to do with the way we behave at home in front of our kids, how to be a parent, how to treat your kids, how to treat each other as spouses. This song is a great example for all of us to follow. Basically, the boy in the song needs his dad who is never there for him, always too busy, always putting things off. His child grows up fast, and when he becomes an adult and the father needs his time, he has no time for him. "My boy was just like me" is how the song closes. It is a remark made by the father, showing the bad consequence of not being there for his son when he needed him.

I think if dads and moms were more aware of the lyrics of this song and their meaning, the song would impact their parenting. I am pretty sure they would make some changes in their behavior.

Another example from the past that has impacted the way I raise my children is the 1988 Tom Hanks movie, *Big*, in which a child becomes an adult overnight. When kids are growing up, they think they want to grow old fast so they can do whatever they want. You see Facebook messages and stuff about children wanting to be on their own. Go ahead and get a job, get a place, do your own laundry, do your own cooking, and so forth, and then you can do whatever you want. *Big* is about a kid who wants to be an adult and it happens. After a having a great time for a while, he realizes he still wants to be a kid.

I saw it from the viewpoint of wanting to be a kid again. I used to tell myself that I hated being an adult because of the responsibilities. I felt that I wanted to go back in time, until I realized I must take responsibility for my own life and move forward. That's the task.

The natural cycle of a baby's development into a child, into a teenager, into a young adult—we should let it happen. We should not wish to control it. If you're a kid, you're a kid. You're going to make mistakes, do all those kinds of things that drive your parents crazy. Do that. Have fun. It's going to be great, and we, as parents, have to understand that.

If you're an adult, you have to take responsibility, but at the same time there's that kid inside you who wants to have fun. The important thing is to remember who is it that you want to be and to be happier with your family and those around you.

I also want to pose to all of you reading this the question of when in your life you really thrived. Think back to that time and how you felt. What were the circumstances that made that time incredible for you?

Just by being myself, being truer to myself, I was happier.

For me, it was when I started my coaching process, when for the first time I began to open up to myself and to everybody else around me. Just by being myself, being truer to myself, I was happier. I was playful and having a great time. I was funny, relaxed, laid back and full of energy and that was me; that was my true self. That was what I found after selling my business. I was able to go into coaching and find the real me.

In addition to coaching, I learned a lot about myself through YPO, the Young Presidents' Organization.

YPO (Young Presidents' Organization) connects you with successful young chief executives in a global network unlike any other. Founded in 1950 in New York City by a young man named Ray Hickok, the organization unites approximately 20,000 business leaders in more than 120 countries around a shared mission: Better Leaders Through Education and Idea Exchange™. Source: YPO website at www.ypo.org.

I have learned a lot from sharing myself with the group and getting to know people from all parts of the world. I see other points of view which I didn't see just working with my father. I see how things can be done in different ways. I have learned to respect others in new ways, to listen to everybody's opinions and ways of doing things, even their ways of being happy, which might be different from my own.

At the same time, the organization has helped me grow, as a person, as a spouse, and as a father. I want to give an example of the parent/child events they have in YPO. Even if people have one kid, I tell them, "Listen, how many times do you spend four days in a row

YOUR RELATIONSHIP WITH FAMILY

just with your son or daughter?" Ninety-nine percent of people will tell me they never spend that alone time with just one of their kids.

Going to a father/daughter or father/son or parent/child event for YPO, and just taking one of your children with you and spending that time together is priceless, and I have done that many times. I am going to another one of these events with one of my daughters this year, and next year I am going to two separate events with my other daughter and with my son. Those are the sort of experiences and memories your kids are going to keep forever. Those are the sorts of moments that you will also always cherish, just being with your kids.

I remember one exercise with one of my daughters when she was ten years old. There were five values and she had to talk about which of the values most related to her and why. Each of the values, of course, was good to have on its own. Listening to my daughter talk about them brought tears to my eyes. She talked about how we connected, and how I raised her, and she did this with a level of depth she didn't often share with me in our daily life.

Such events allow you to spend time with your kids. Reflect on that time and share it. Cherish what you have. Sometimes we take for granted what we have, even our own kids, and then we expect them to be perfect. This sharing, this exercise, really helped me better understand my own family dynamics.

One thing I want to stress to all of you out there is to not hide behind work, using it as an excuse to not be with those you love.

One thing I want to stress to all of you out there is to not hide behind work, using it as an excuse to not be with those you love or

CHAPTER TEN

Work-Life Balance

I found many of my secrets to work-life balance in the retreats and classes I have attended. I get support from the people around me, who help me learn more about myself. Yet, maybe you're saying to yourself as you read this book, "Easy enough for you, Jofi." And granted I know it is easy to do that when you're with like-minded people and can benefit from the support structure of a personal growth retreat.

However, once you go back home after a training course, especially after being in a group like the Hoffman Process, it's completely different. It's a little more work. The training and learning process that I took about a month before I started my coaching training was an eight-day, personal growth retreat. They told us to prepare ourselves because as hopeful and energetic as we might have become during that time, when we went back home, the world would not have changed.

You've changed, sure, but the world is still the same as you left it eight days ago. It's not going to be the same to go back home and be yourself. It's going to take a little bit more work, and for me, going through my coaching training was a great process. Overall, it actually took a little bit more than a year to really start rediscovering who I was. Who am I? What do I want to do with my life? What moves me?

What's my passion? What makes me happy?—and to move forward with my life.

What moves me? What's my passion? What makes me happy?

My parents always made me feel that I had everything that I needed, and I never wanted for material things. I know this is true, but sometimes I wasn't happy, based on the fact that even with all the material things I had, I still didn't know what to do with myself. I didn't know me. Let's put it that way. I had not found myself.

Through all this training I did for my coaching in New Ventures West, and the personal growth retreat I attended with the Hoffman Process, I found out who I was. I found out what I wanted to do with my life. I found what makes me happy, and it's a process. It's a daily process. We all need to become aware of what it is that makes us come alive. Just as I said earlier, it makes me so happy to talk about somebody else and recommend that person for a job. It is something that seems so simple. It makes me happy to help people.

It makes me happy coaching people and knowing that I make a difference in other people's lives.

It makes me happy coaching people and knowing that I make a difference in other people's lives. Understanding myself better helps me to be happier and at the same time it helps everybody who's in contact with me: my kids, my friends, my family—everybody. That's what I want to share with you as you read this book.

I'll give an example from a book that's very popular at the moment, *50 Shades of Grey*. I have started reading books I might not normally read, just to see what is in them, especially as I travel so much and can use the flight time to read. I was looking in the airport for books when I spied *50 Shades of Grey* behind the cashier. I decided to see what so many people were talking about.

One of the main characters, Mr. Christian Grey, is a very successful, good looking, young guy. He has everything that would seem positive in life. Anastasia, the other character, talks about how she likes playful Christian, and how wonderful it is to be near him when he is in a playful mood. Looking at myself as I read the book, I realize I like playful joking too. I think we all like the funny guy, the guy who's relaxed, the guy who is always joking. Christian is open and fun. He's not a stiff, not a snob, when in his playful mood. You can see the appeal in the character.

What the book made me realize is that I love it when I am relaxed, laid back, and having fun. I think when my mind is free of any bad thoughts, any pressure or stress—because I'm learning to handle those better—I am me. I am myself. I am funnier, more playful, more relaxed, and all that makes me aware that that's who I want to be.

When my wife and I talk about our marriage and when I met her, she mentions I was always funny, making her laugh. That was why she decided I was the one for her. Now, I look back and I say, "Oh, that's what it was." That was the real me. I think, as we got older, and I entered the business world, I got sucked into being a more serious person because, after all, I was the boss. I think through coaching, through learning how to find myself, I realized what was lost over the years. This is the value I believe I bring into my coaching practice, helping people return to their real selves, something that might have been lost over time as we get old, join the work force, and focus on money rather than the relationships that made us happy.

I realize, now, I am the person I love to be. Who am I? My training to be a coach has been part of who I am. With that behind me I am learning more about myself even as I write the book you have in your hands. I am more aware of what motivates me. I am moved by helping people find meaning or happiness, or whatever it is that they need in their lives. I want to share my experiences doing this in this book. This is one of the main reasons I decided I wanted to help other people out there: I want to help them come to the decisions they need to make in order to have a better life for themselves.

You may not relate to everything I have been saying, or maybe to just a part of it, or maybe to most of it. The important thing is that various components of what is in here, in this book, in my story, can really help make a significant, positive, impactful change in your life—the way they did in mine.

WHERE I AM NOW

All of this background, and all of these chapters to this point are to tell you who I am and how I got here—all the things that have made me who I am, have brought me to where I am today, what made me decide to be a coach.

The interesting thing about coaching is that a coach is not there to tell you what to do. The coach is going to guide you, and help you to find out for yourself. That way it's going to have a long-term impact, and there will be a permanent change in you. If I tell you what to do right now, you probably will do it, but eventually you will forget, and you will actually not get what it is you need to be looking for, the change you need to find in yourself.

I think sometimes we get lazy, and we want the answer right away, and I have learned through my own experience that this coaching process works because it goes deeper. Two and a half years into my training to be a coach, I am still going through a lot of stuff. I understand now how it works, and how the changes I am making are based on what I felt I needed to do. I feel more secure making that decision on my own, rather than doing it because someone tells me to. Instead, I did it because I was able to look inside myself and know it was the right thing to do. Through this self-knowledge, this self-awareness, you realize what you should do is obvious. It is what you feel is right, based on all of your research, the way you feel, the things you know about yourself.

Coaching really helps you with your own issues and helps you build confidence. When you are coached, you build yourself inside, because it's you who is doing everything. It's you who's doing all the work.

When you are coached, you build yourself inside, because it's you who is doing everything. It's you who's doing all the work.

Everything I've done in my life adds to who I am today. All of this I want to share with you, the reader, and with everyone else who might benefit and learn from my experiences. Hopefully, all my readers will get something out of it.

There are no three easy steps to do this, or seven ways to be happy. Coaching is not that kind of simplified self-help process. I am no self-proclaimed guru. There are, of course, certain things you must do. For some people some things work, for others, they don't. But who decides, in the end?

IT'S YOU WHO DECIDES

I think that's one of the main messages I want to send in this book. It's about you and how you are going to decide your work-life balance. How are you going to integrate all that in your life? What is comfortable for you?

No one can say being home early three days a week, or just one day a week, is perfect for you, because you work too much, or travel too much, or whatever it is that might be in the way—your own personal obstacles. It's only you who can decide that.

There's no right or wrong. Sometimes we live as if there is a right way and a wrong way, some model we must follow. I ask why. Recently, in a positive psychology class, Tal, my professor, mentioned the rules.

The rules are about being on time and being respectful of others in class. This is what you would expect, but he did an interesting thing. He said, "I know it's going to happen and people are going to be late and that's fine." He added, "That's okay. Just be aware and give yourself permission to be human." I think sometimes we are too hard on ourselves. We're always looking for that perfect life. We think we should be perfect, and we get frustrated when we don't follow through with everything. As we all know, no one's perfect. There are rules, but there are times when we cannot follow them all, when something gets in the way. Life is like that.

And for me personally, as a perfectionist, it has taken me a long time to realize this. Maybe I beat myself up and then I realize, well that's a mistake I made and I'm just going to learn from it. We cannot all be perfect; we can only try to be perfect, and actually, we should not even try. Learning from mistakes along the way is what is important.

I'd Like to Point Out to You Some Famous Successes Who Started Out as Failures.

Few would doubt Michael Jordan is one of the greatest basketball players in all of the world. But did you know that when he did not make his high-school basketball team, Michael Jordan went to a room and started crying?

What about another famously successful failure? The late Steve Jobs of Apple once said he was depressed when he was thirty years old, because he was fired from the company he had built. Imagine that now: fired from the company he had built. But he rejoined the company, of course, bringing it through its greatest period of revival and success.

Oh, and another: Walt Disney was fired from a newspaper he was working for because he didn't have enough imagination. He was told that he didn't have any original ideas. Now, of course, everyone wishes to emulate Walt Disney, one of the most creative geniuses ever to grace this planet.

I can give you another example—from the world of media—an iconic television goddess, Oprah Winfrey. Years ago, Oprah Winfrey was fired from her job as a reporter because she didn't know how to work in front of a TV camera—yes, Oprah Winfrey!

But from Failures, One Learns to Be Successful

It's one of those things I learned myself, the hard way. I need to be able to go ahead and know it's not going to be perfect. For example, my website is not finished, and I have no idea when it will be finished. I know this, because it's me who has to decide to finish it. Waiting for perfection has paralyzed the process, and I need to make a decision soon. I will do my best to have it finished by the time the book comes out.

I have also learned about the "good-enough" theory and about being different. If I want to be a great writer, I might read Shakespeare, or Conrad, or Hemingway, in a way to determine what makes them great. It doesn't mean that it's going to make me great also. What I should try to do is take the good from whatever they are doing and see what works and doesn't work for me in what I am writing.

And that is not just about words and form, but about doing your best at whatever you do. I know people who are night owls. They can't get clear thoughts until the sun has gone down, until the day has settled away. Some writers might work best from midnight to 5:00 a.m., and they might be the best writers in the world. Maybe these writers found the ideal time for them to write. That's when the ideas come to them, when they are more creative.

So what is the right time for me? What is the most creative time for me? What are my most productive hours?

Well, if I am a morning person, rising early at 5:00 a.m. and writing, say, until 8:00 a.m., before the world gets busy—my quiet, thoughtful, writing time—I am going to use that time, not some other writer's time. Model others' behaviors. Learn from others, but do it in a way that works for you.

Model others' behaviors. Learn from others,
but do it in a way that works for you.

Truly, for me, it's the morning that is best. As an example, I am here writing and working at 7:30 a.m. I did some work with my positive psychology, and I got ready for more time with this book, with my head and thoughts clear and focused.

Everyone has to be aware of his or her own best time. It's not because it worked for someone else it's supposed to work for you. You have to be aware of that. I learned about meditation through my coaching training. I think a lot of people never stop to take a break, basically a mental break. Meditation helps you take that break, the mental break, and just be there with whatever comes up.

It's not about making it happen. It's not about expectations. It's not about anything. It's just a time for you to be there meditating with whatever comes up, and that's it. We can talk about many types of meditation, but it's basically a simple mental break you give to yourself.

The important thing when trying to be happy is that you can't shoot immediately for a perfect work-life balance. There's no such thing as perfect. Shoot for something that you can reasonably do. Do it step by step. You make the transition. You find what works for you.

You start to become happy with it, and along the way, you make the necessary changes or twists to it that you need to make, whatever it takes to find your happy self.

Finding Your Happy Self

We're at the end of the book, and I am glad you have joined me on this journey.

While I know that, for each of us, it can be something different, I want to talk about what a happy life looks like. Find out what makes you happy, all while understanding there's no magic pill or magic secret for happiness. I can mention a lot of ideas that may help to increase your happiness, and I already have, throughout this book, but I know it will work differently for each person.

You know that even if I were to suggest to you a hundred and one ways to be happier, you cannot implement them all. You're never going to be able to do a hundred and one things, and by following such a rule, so to speak, you're not going to be happier. Instead, you should be able to pick what's going to work for you, based on your feelings and your timing. You need to understand that it is all up to you.

To be happy, you cannot blame your boss; you cannot blame the weather; you cannot blame your spouse, your kids, or anyone else in your life. At the end of the day the one responsible is you.

I can understand that you might get mad when you are with someone, or when it's a cloudy day, you become sad. Yet, it's up to you, no one else, to decide what to do about your emotions. The first thing to be aware of is how you are feeling, and then you must decide how you are going to act based on that knowledge. It is up to you. You make the next move, no one else. You have to be self-aware and then be able to make the necessary changes to get to the place where you want to be—happiness and fulfillment, or whatever it is you want. What is your goal? Is it taking a different attitude to those people whose company makes you mad, or having a more relaxed view of the weather, no matter whether it's sunny or stormy? You have to realize that how you react to different situations is what is important. How you react to your own emotions is up to you.

Questions that you can ask yourself are: What makes you happy? What makes you come alive? Is it writing? Is it speaking in public? Is it spending time with your family? Is it going swimming, running, watching a good movie, just hanging out reading a good book? Whatever the answer is for you—emphasis on *you*—try to do more of it.

There's the classic example of how you start your day. A lot of people start their day watching the news. What do you see in the news? Bad news, crime, stress, this and that. You start your day in a negative way. Are you bringing that anxiety with you to work, or to your family? Try to be aware of that.

Nowadays, our lives can be too busy. We're trying to do too many things. And doing too many things all at once can not only be frustrating, it can also make us dumber. There is research on this. Research done by a group of psychologists at the University of London (Glen Wilson, 2005) tells us that texting or e-mailing while doing work that requires concentration is equal to losing ten IQ points.

And doing too many things all at once can not only be frustrating, it can also make us dumber.

It's true even if it sounds hard to believe, because after all, don't we strive to be multitaskers, getting more done at the same time? Leslie Perlow's 1999 study about "time famine" finds that the introduction of uninterrupted quiet time in the workplace increases productivity and well-being. Basically, the message is that less is more. We're trying to do too many things and it just doesn't work. We're not achieving anything, even though sometimes we feel we have to do more. Did you ever feel each task takes you longer because you're trying to do two things at once, whereas maybe doing one thing at a time would not only be less frustrating but perhaps save time overall?

There are so many other stories that I can tell, but one I definitely want to relate is from one of my YPO events. At the meeting, one guy told me about how good and relaxed I looked. He wanted the formula. What makes me seem relaxed is simply that I find my own way to happiness. I thought about all the things I could tell him, but he needed to find his own formula. And that formula certainly wasn't about obtaining more money in his life. It's already been proven that, beyond having money for basic needs, money does not contribute to happiness.

What makes me seem relaxed is simply that I find my own way to happiness.

We actually need what Perlow calls "time affluence"—wealth of time —which is, basically, the feeling that we have the time to do whatever it is that we want to do. Time affluence is a better predictor of well-being than material affluence.

Of course, often, one of the things that takes away from our time affluence is the inability to say no. To help others, you say yes to everybody at work, at charities, and in the end, the person you're saying no to is yourself. You have given so much time to others that, in the end, you have no time for yourself.

You have given so much time to others that, in the end, you have no time for yourself.

We need to start working on living a simpler life. We need to work on the optimum levels of simplicity needed to be happier because we have to be able to enjoy whatever it is that we're trying to do. I will give you this analogy. Two of my favorite songs right now are *Looking for Paradise* by Alejandro Sanz, featuring Alicia Keys, and *Tengo Tu Love* by Sie7e. If I give each song a ten, does that mean I get a twenty if I put them together?

No. Life today, is about scale: trying to work while checking e-mail, texting, thinking about this and that, trying to do too many things. Perlow has this theory that instead of looking for the perfect life, we should look for the good-enough life. Adding more does not give you more. We sometimes need to forgo perfection to find happiness, something we have long been told is not true, which is why, at the beginning, this theory shocked me. Good enough? It's kind of like you're not doing your best, but you're basically shifting from perfect to good enough, and that shift will take you from frustration to satisfaction.

Good enough I think is important as a concept. We need to have an understanding that perfection, or always wanting perfection, is a form of procrastination. We also have a fear of presenting things to people before they are "perfect," and that in itself means we never get things done. What I will say is that perfection puts me on hold. It puts me on hold because in my pursuit of perfection I never finish anything. Then I never move forward.

I haven't met anybody who is perfect. We should give ourselves permission to be human. We should give permission to be human to other people with whom we interact. And that will help, in the end, in your well-being and your pursuit of happiness.

> ## *We should give permission to be human to other people with whom we interact.*

As an example, let's say we have two columns on a piece of paper. One is our perfect life; the other is what we know we can achieve. In a perfect life, you will have six date nights a week with your wife. No one has that much time! Well, as an example, my wife and I both have work, the kids, so our date night is once a week. Even that has some constraints. We have changed the day of the week to suit our schedules. It's not perfect, but we still achieve it. That's the goal.

Let's see another thing. Maybe, in a perfect life, we hang out with friends three or four times a week. In a good-enough life, maybe we hang out once a week. Spending time with kids every day is perfect, but in a good-enough life, you spend two or three days a week in the afternoon and all day Saturday with them. This is more realistic considering you need time to work and make a living. At the same time, it's a more realistic schedule because you don't frustrate yourself; you're not trying to be perfect or trying to achieve something that is not possible. When you do this, everybody wins.

WHAT COACHING MEANS TO ME

I want to share what worked for me in coaching and what I love to do. For me coaching is work, from the point of view that it made me work on myself. For some reason I never really had to work on myself before. Through coaching, for the first time, I looked inside myself, a deep introspection.

What was I going to do about how I felt? What was going to move me and my career path—everything? The effect that it had was life altering for me. I took the steps that I felt were right for me, for example, becoming a coach myself after having worked with other coaches. In my society and among my group of friends this was seen as very different, something strange—you know—because people get fixed ideas about what a job should be about, what a corporate office and all those things that come with it should look like, or what owning a business or starting a new one should be about.

Their attitude was something I had to deal with. When you talk to a lot of people who have no idea what a coach is, it's kind of like "Wow!" you know. They look at you with this funny face that seems to ask, "What the heck did you get yourself into?" Again people have a fixed idea of what work should look like. They listen to these outer voices. Not the one that matters, their inner voice.

> ## *They listen to these outer voices.*
> ## *Not the one that matters, their inner voice.*

I really believe in what I'm doing, and I know the changes I have helped people see in themselves give me the strength to move forward. I'm looking forward to speaking about what I do as a coach. When I speak, when I write—all of those things—that is what I love to do. That is what moves me. That is what makes me come to life.

I have to be aware of that, and I know it helps me come alive. I know it helps me become a better father. I know it helps me become a better husband because I'm doing what makes me happy. At the same time because of what I do, I learn much more about myself.

I'm continually learning about life, about the human state of being, from all my clients, from all the people with whom I interact. It really has had, and continues to have, a big impact on me.

I was one of those people who liked to tell others what to do. I was a boss, after all. But among the things I learned in the coaching process is that most often, when people tell you what to do in terms of personal advice, especially when it is unsolicited, they are doing it out of kindness and concern. They don't necessarily mean any harm. Think of your aunt, or a best friend, who worries. That person has your best interests at heart.

But you know what? First off, it's probably not a good idea to do that. Second, the best way to help is to share your own experiences of what you went through and what you learned from them so other people can take from it whatever they feel might work for them. Explain, give an example, or several, and take it from there. Let the other person decide.

I think we should go through life looking at it this way: What can I learn from this situation? What can I learn from that person?

Stopping and thinking about our actions will help us make the decisions that lead us to a better, more fulfilling, happier life. Think about where you are now. Think about where you want to go. Do you have a plan for your life, or do you just say, "I'm going to work and take care of my family"?

Let's go into more detail. What does *work* mean? What does *take care of your family* mean?

Do you want to save some money for your kids' college education, or are they going to get a scholarship, or are they going to get financial aid? Do you want to work to save money for this special trip with your wife, with your family? What is it that you want to get out of this life? What is it that you would like to accomplish?

What is it that you want to get out of this life?

How are you going to raise your kids? Are you and your spouse on the same page about how to raise them? What are your expectations for them when they become adults?

If you don't talk and think about those things, who is going to do that for you? Think about it. Who is going to do that for you? I share credit in this book with others who have pointed things out to me, including Tal, those in YPO who have really helped guide me through my life, my mother, and others. I wrote my values down, and I read them almost every day. My motto, my credo, is right next to my computer. I become aware of my values, what I think of, what I believe, and that gives me a way of checking into my own value system.

My credo is checking on me all the time to make sure I am following the path I chose for myself, not somebody else's path, not the path described in books, but what I actually chose to do myself. My values are a combination of what I have gathered from my own experiences, what I have learned from other people, what I have gathered from books I have read, and what I have learned from all the interactions I have had with different people all over the world. In the end, though, the beliefs are my own, all my own.

That's why I invited you, the reader, to come up with your own set of values, your own credo. I think you're going to be very happy and surprised at the outcome of these exercises.

And creating a credo can be life changing in so many other ways. Examining my values has meant a big change in my life, in which I went from the insurance business, where it meant wearing a jacket and tie every day, to the other side of the spectrum.

Now, I go to work in jeans. And for shirts? Actually, I wear guayaberas from Panama, where my wife is from, and I'm very comfortable with this. I go to most of my functions dressed like this. If I want to dress up a little bit, I wear a long-sleeved shirt. If I want to take it a step further, I change to pants and another type of shirt.

The interesting thing is that before we sold the company, I barely ever wore jeans, let alone at work. The other day it hit me that it's been a while since I really dressed up, not just in a jacket and tie, but really dressed up, looking good for an event, and I asked myself if this was something that I should do.

Then I answered myself: It's nice to do once in a while whenever I feel like it, but it's not something I need. For me it was a surprise when I realized, "Wow! It's been a while since I've dressed up, whereas, normally, that was my order of the day, being all dressed up."

It means I'm becoming more myself. I'm finding the me I am comfortable with. And that is a wonderful feeling.

I'm finding the me I am comfortable with.
And that is a wonderful feeling.

I will give you another example, this time from a formal business lunch award ceremony here in Puerto Rico. I knew everybody was going to be wearing a jacket and tie. I decided, "Well, I will not go in jeans but I'll just go in dress pants and a long-sleeved shirt." When I got there, I was shocked. I had forgotten that everyone else would be in a dark suit.

Still, I was fine with it. I saw a few people in sports jackets because they felt they had to wear them. I saw how uncomfortable they were. They didn't look good because the sports jackets were not what they were about.

I saw this expresident of my bank. He was much taller than I was, so he rose above everyone else in the room. He looked at me and began to move closer. "Jofi, you know what?" He was all in his jacket and tie, looking very professional. He tugged at his tie, as if it were too tight, and he said, "I wanted to come dressed just like you are, but I didn't have the balls to do it." Almost conspiratorially, with a smile, I said, "Well, next time, you call me, and we'll come together. You'll feel comfortable."

I was glad he was able to tell me this.

Look, if I know I really need to be in a jacket and tie, I will wear a jacket and tie. I know right from wrong, and I have the ability to rise to the occasion. I'm not saying I'm not going to do that, and I'm not suggesting you dress up any way you want to for certain specific functions, disobeying dress codes. No, that's not the point I am trying to make here. I have decided that this is for me. When I come to work, I can do that because of the kind of work I'm doing now, and because this is my decision. This is what I chose, and I feel comfortable with it. There's nothing wrong with that. But it took a long time for me to be able to feel this way.

This is the way I dress now and for the work I do, I can. If you work in a bank or anywhere with the public, you might have a dress code to follow. In my type of work it doesn't really matter what I wear. The important thing is the ability to impact change in people. That has nothing to do with how I am dressed, or what fashion labels or suits I am wearing, or what I look like. It's about the impact I have on someone's feelings through my words and actions, through the plan we have formed together for how that person is going to change his or her life. It is not about my suit and tie.

BECOMING A COACH

Sometimes this switch from a "real" job, as so many people call it, to becoming a coach, seems a difficult thing to wrap one's head around. Yet, as a business person, as a good leader, you help people figure it out at work all the time. I am not talking about telling people what to do, but rather, guiding them in making the right decisions, so they take ownership of those decisions. That's being a great work leader, director, president, boss. Being a good coach entails the same principles. We are not pointing out to people things they need to do. There is definitely a negative aspect to that. Instead, a good coach tries to make people be cognizant of how they're doing things and of the decisions they're making on a day-to-day basis.

A good coach tries to make people be cognizant of how they're doing things and of the decisions they're making on a day-to-day basis.

Are those decisions the right decisions for them? And if they thought a little bit more about their day and about some of their decisions, would they be more efficient? Would they be happier? These are the things that a coach does and thinks about. This is what I learned from doing what a coach does. Even on my own, as a coach, I learn every day from my clients.

I realized, when I was being coached, I had the calling to also be a coach. When I talk to people about what I'm doing, I come across many people who would like to do that same thing. They feel they have that calling, and they tell me that once they know they have the time to change their lives and do something else, coaching is something they really would like to do.

I think it comes to the point where sometimes we are in careers that no longer bring, or perhaps never have brought, meaning into our lives. The human being in a natural state is very giving and caring. By coaching, you're helping others become, overcome, reach—whatever it is they're working on.

You're bringing meaning to other people out there and that, in turn, brings you meaning.

At the same time, as you're coaching and helping others, you're actually helping yourself because you're bringing meaning to other people out there and that, in turn, brings you meaning. Your own well-being improves; your happiness improves; and your sense of fulfillment improves, because you're doing work with true value and meaning. You're doing something with a positive impact in this world we're living in today. I think more of that is necessary to live a happy, healthier life.

The satisfaction that I get from helping others, as a coach, is something immeasurable. It's something that spreads because the more fulfilled I feel, the more meaningful my work becomes. This is a self-feeding cycle, in which the happier I am, the more that happiness spreads to those around me. The experience of every person I come in contact with is more positive. They feel more fulfilled than before.

The phrase *fill the bucket* means you add to people's lives, you fill their "buckets." On the other hand, the phrase *take away from the bucket* means you take away from people's lives, you rob their "buckets." Fill the bucket, that's what I do in every interaction I have with each one of my clients.

This sounds as if it involves money, but it really means that being negative takes something away from the other person in the interaction. When you fill other people's bucket, you bring happy, positive energy to them. How are you with people? How are some people around you? Have you trained yourself to be around those who fill your bucket, avoiding those who take away? The question to ask yourself is whether you fill other people's buckets in every inter-action you have with other human beings. Do you add something positive to them, or do you take away from their buckets? I look at it that way, and in every interaction I have with somebody, I ask myself how I am behaving, how I am interacting with that person. I want to give value to other people's lives through my own.

Have you trained yourself to be around those who fill your bucket, avoiding those who take away?

How do you fill someone's bucket? It can be very simple. Do you say good morning and give a smile to the cashier at the supermarket, at the drug store, at the gas station? That's who I am, and that is what I strive to do every day.

Now It's Your Turn: Find Your "Happy Self"

This book presents my story—what I learned on my journey to find my "happy self." I've shared this "unwritten" story in the hope that it will make a positive impact on your life.

What is your "unwritten" story? I encourage you to take a minute to think about the life you are living. Now, think about the life you *want* to live.

Ask yourself:

- Am I living my life on cruise control?
- What do I really want?
- What makes me happy?
- What small thing can I do, right now, to live a happier, more meaningful life?

As a coach, I guide teenagers, young adults, business owners and successful adults to investigate these nagging questions. Working as a team with each coaching client, we identify personal values, clarify his or her path, and set specific and exciting life goals. Fueled by a compelling goal, they wake up excited to "get to work" every day.

They are not adrift—they have a direction. And they live a life full of passion, meaning, and purpose.

I truly believe you can live a life of passion, meaning, and purpose. And you can be happy. I encourage you to continue your journey to find your "happy self."

Un abrazo,
Jofi

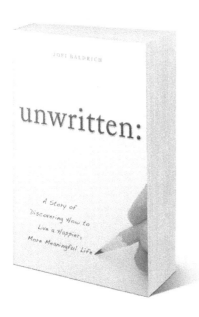

How can you use this book?

MOTIVATE

EDUCATE

THANK

INSPIRE

PROMOTE

CONNECT

Why have a custom version of *Unwritten*?

- Build personal bonds with customers, prospects, employees, donors, and key constituencies
- Develop a long-lasting reminder of your event, milestone, or celebration
- Provide a keepsake that inspires change in behavior and change in lives
- Deliver the ultimate "thank you" gift that remains on coffee tables and bookshelves
- Generate the "wow" factor

Books are thoughtful gifts that provide a genuine sentiment that other promotional items cannot express. They promote employee discussions and interaction, reinforce an event's meaning or location, and they make a lasting impression. Use your book to say "Thank You" and show people that you care.

Unwritten is available in bulk quantities and in customized versions at special discounts for corporate, institutional, and educational purposes. To learn more please contact our Special Sales team at:

1.866.775.1696 • sales@advantageww.com • www.AdvantageSpecialSales.com